Grammar

for Improving Reading and Writing in the Secondary School

Geoff Dean

David Fulton Publishers
London

David Fulton Publishers Ltd
The Chiswick Centre, 414 Chiswick High Road, London W4 5TF

www.fultonpublishers.co.uk

David Fulton Publishers is a division of Granada Learning Ltd, part of the
Granada Media group.

First published 2003
10 9 8 7 6 5 4 3 2 1

Copyright © 2003 Geoff Dean

British Library Cataloguing in Publication Data
A catalogue record for this book is available from the British Library.

ISBN 1 84312 003 8

Typeset by Textype, Cambridge
Printed and bound in Scotland by Scotprint, Haddington

August 28, 2008

Contents

A Short Grammar

Three little words you often see
Are Articles, A, An and The.

A Noun is the name of Anything,
As School or Garden, Hoop or Swing.

Adjectives tell the kind of Noun,
As Great, Small, Pretty, White or Brown.

Instead of Nouns the Pronouns stand –
His head, Her face, Your arm, My hand.

Verbs tell something to be done –
To Read, Count, Laugh, Sing, Jump or Run.

How things are done the Adverbs tell –
As Slowly, Quickly, Ill or Well.

Conjunctions join the words together
As men And women, wind Or weather.

The Preposition stands before
The nouns as In or Through the door.

The Interjection shows surprise –
As Oh! how pretty, Ah! how wise.

The whole are called nine parts of speech,
Which Reading, Writing, Speaking teach.

A traditional anonymous view of language teaching at the beginning of the 1900s, contributed by my Aunty Jan (who is pleased to see grammar teaching returning to English studies!)

Acknowledgements

To the teachers who made learning language such fun:

Peter Hewitt
Neil Salmon
Geoff Mitchell
George Keith

Thank you.

Acknowledgements are gratefully made to:

Hodder Children's books for extracts from *Skellig* by David Almond and *heathrow nights* by Jan Mark; Doubleday for extracts from *Remembrance* by Theresa Breslin; Penguin Books for extracts from *Stone Cold* by Robert Swindells; *Radio Times* and *Good Housekeeping* for extracts.

The publishers acknowledge permission to use extracts from the following poems:

'Brother' (p.119) – Mary Ann Hoberman – Little Brown & Co; Gina Maccoby Literacy Agency
'The Horse' (p.119) – Edwin Muir – Faber & Faber
'Hawk Roosting' (p.120) – Ted Hughes – Faber & Faber
'Oh What is that Sound?' (p.120) – W. H. Auden – Faber & Faber
'Do Not Go Gentle into that Good Night' (p.120) – Dylan Thomas
'The Oxen' (p.121) – Thomas Hardy – Macmillan
'One Flesh' (p.119) – Elizabeth Jennings – Macmillan
'The Magic Box' (p.124) – Kit Wright – Viking Kestrel

Introduction

I am not a linguist. I have neither trained in or studied linguistics, nor have I undertaken research in grammar or related areas of learning. I was taught 'grammar' in the English lessons of my grammar school, and I have found out about and read a number of materials dealing with language because of my links with the National Literacy Strategy. Through these contacts I discovered that the topic has the potential to be increasingly fascinating. If only I had known a fraction of what I know now about this topic when I was teaching English: it would have made a considerable positive difference to my teaching and my pupils' learning. If I have made any major mistakes in the advice I offer, or if specialist teachers of language are offended about my lack of scholarship, I can only apologise. However, this was never meant to be a scholarly textbook. It claims to be no more than a helpful source of ideas and approaches to language study, as a way of digging deeper into the meanings of the textual materials pupils deal with every day in their English (and other) lessons.

The best place to begin any study of grammar is by enjoying some fun with real text. Grammar, at least in the way we should regard it in schools, only really 'exists' as text – when it comes into its own as those ways in which words rub up against each other to become discourses with particular purposes. Much of the evidence on the teaching of grammar suggests that it is not worth bothering with unless pupils begin to see it not as an end in itself, but as a valuable apparatus to examine texts more thoroughly, and to create them with greater control and power (Harrison 2002; Hilton 2001; Mittins, 1988).

Teachers, in introducing this area of English work to a Key Stage 3 class, might select any accessible (but not necessarily easy) text and set about exploring with their pupils how the author has conveyed meaning through using patterns or combinations of language in particular and deliberately chosen ways. Some texts are 'great friends' to teachers in this situation, offering excellent examples of the sorts of knowledge pupils can acquire readily, while being substantially interesting and engaging for a range of readers.

Anthony Browne's very clever picture book *Voices in the Park* (1998) is an excellent starting point for such an exploration. This story is itself a development of an earlier text, *A Walk in the Park* (1977), published some 20 years earlier. (Teachers keen to promote the learning of reading and writing, and the craft of authorship, will be asking their pupils to compare the two texts in appropriate ways in a separate context.) Four characters, or 'voices', are involved in the simplest of plots: a walk in the park by a mother and her son, a father and his daughter, and two dogs. Yet each of the human characters tells his or her own version of the narrative, from his or her own point of view, in a manner utterly characteristic of each individual, portrayed in the language of each of the 'voices', with the pictures 'confirming' those four different linguistic viewpoints.

Two of the characters are adults, and two are children: a middle-class mother and her son; a working-class father and his daughter. It should be made perfectly clear that the written language is not the only vehicle for conveying meaning in this text. The detailed, often surrealistic, vivid pictures accompanying each 'voice' denote much about that protagonist, as do the quite different individual fonts in which their narratives are related. These layers of meaning work together to confirm and complement each other perfectly, allowing pupils to see how deliberately the meanings can be made. Because a few pupils may encounter difficulties with the linguistic issues being explored in this exercise, the Browne text is particularly appropriate. Everyone should be able to draw some conclusions about the various characters given the many layers of meaning contained within this book.

I recommend an approach to the written text called 'close textual study', explained in more detail by the linguist George Keith in his chapter 'Noticing grammar' in the QCA booklet *Not Whether But How* (QCA 1999), and developed further in my book *Teaching Reading in Secondary Schools* (2000). This technique involves paying close attention to short sections of text, often individual words, but certainly not much more than phrases, to 'problematise' every part; i.e. to raise intensely focused questions about those sections. This approach means that the reader is expected to attempt to explain why particular linguistic choices have been made in the writing, to open up a short discussion about such things as what the 'functions' of the language might be, the likely possible effects, associations and ultimate authorial intent.

The woman's narrative begins:

It was time to take Victoria, our pedigree Labrador, and Charles, our son, for a walk.

The man's begins:

> I needed to get out of the house, so me and Smudge took the dog to the park.

The beginning of the boy's version is:

> I was at home on my own again. It's so boring. Then Mummy said that it was time for our walk. There was a very friendly dog in the park and Victoria was having a great time. I wished I was.

The girl's story begins:

> Dad had been really fed up, so I was pleased when he said we could take Albert to the park.

Pupils, in small groups, should be urged (or – perhaps more realistically in the introductory stage – coached) to begin their close investigation. The first words of each passage should already spark certain insights: the woman's 'It was time' suggests somebody who is ruled by and makes a ritual of events, a 'control freak' in modern parlance! She does not question the events of her day; the rule-governed life she leads is absolute (and is echoed and confirmed directly in her son's subsequent version). Two of the other three accounts begin with the **pronoun** 'I', pointing to a more self-absorbed attitude on the part of the narrator, while the first word of the girl's story is 'Dad', raising the likelihood of a more caring, philanthropic nature because of her attention to someone else.

So, in the first narrative, what was it 'time' for? The woman continues:

> to take Victoria, our pedigree Labrador, and Charles, our son, for a walk.

This sentence reveals a wealth of consistent detail. First, it is a perfect piece of **Standard English**; studiously correct in every respect. The **nouns** are important: 'Victoria' and 'Charles' suggest a clearly identifiable level of society that she inhabits; and they both have an association with royalty. This royal connection is made even more explicit in two distinct ways. Later in the text the reader discovers that the mongrel daring to 'bother' to play with Victoria is (ironically?) named 'Albert'! The woman also refers to Victoria unselfconsciously as 'our pedigree Labrador', and Charles as 'our son'; examples of the 'royal we'. The use of these **pronouns** in this context has long been associated with the historical manner in which English monarchs, or certain pretentious commoners, refer to themselves. It is also likely to remind many readers of the famous moment when Margaret Thatcher, then Prime Minister, danced down the steps of No. 10 Downing Street, announcing, 'We are a grandmother!'

The references to 'Victoria, our pedigree Labrador', and 'Charles, our son', have further significance, however. They are examples of **nouns in apposition**; that is, an instance where two nouns, or a noun and a noun phrase are juxtaposed, both with the same meaning – yet where the second use explains the first reference more explicitly. This deliberate, almost choking precision suggested in her nature would seem to be wholly consistent with the 'it was time' introduction. (Fully confirmed, incidentally, by the pictures drawn to represent her in the accompanying illustrations.) It could also be claimed that her insistent requirement to be so exact in her narrative is a way of patronising her audience: those attending to her narrative cannot be trusted to reach the correct interpretation without her total guidance. One further point of interest in this sentence is the order of the **nouns**: the dog clearly has precedence over the son! And this is not a chance assertion; Browne deliberately repeats the order later in her narrative to drive the message home. This paragraph, concerned with revealing the particular characteristics of this central protagonist, would not be complete without some reference to her obvious use of the ostentatious **adjective** 'pedigree' before the **noun** 'Labrador'. The reader is left in no doubt about the utterly pukka background of the dog; pointedly compared in the space of only two more sentences with a 'scruffy mongrel' belonging to the other family in the story.

This 'mongrel' causes the woman enormous consternation:

> When we arrived at the park, I let Victoria off her lead. Immediately some scruffy mongrel appeared and started bothering her. I shooed it off, but the horrible thing chased her all over the park.

By being perfectly serious in the way she relates her story, this character unconsciously provides moments of delicious comedy! Her **euphemism** 'started bothering her' contains a whole puritan set of proper social conventions – to be challenged directly at a later stage by the girl's interpretation of the same moment. It is followed by the **verbs** 'shooed' and 'chased', both representing a personal sense of what is taking place, fully consistent with the ways she has presented herself to the readers of the text. The mindset of this woman we have been offered, through the medium of her own language, refuses to recognise that Victoria could possibly be enjoying this experience, and far from being 'chased' she is indulging herself fully. The **adjective** 'horrible' attached to the **noun** 'thing' also says much about her. She thinks she is being forthright in using such a term, but in actual fact she seems very tame and lacks any real explicitness in such a bland description.

If some of the interpretation offered about the woman seems a little forced at first acquaintance, comparison with the second character should reassure the sceptical reader that every detail was intended.

I needed to get out of the house, so me and Smudge took the dog to the park.

The beginnings are clearly contrasted: 'It was time' has already been considered carefully, but while the woman works to fixed routines, and appears remotely at some distance from the events of her life, the man is compelled into action. Attention to the **verbs** in the groups of words 'it was time' and 'I needed to' makes such contrasts explicit. The first voice is controlled, detached and passive – the second is immediate and utterly active. Thus, through this simple contrasting device readers are offered two wholly different characters, leading their lives from diametrically opposite motivations. This second character pays less attention to the correct grammatical construction of this first-person narrative: 'so me and Smudge took the dog to the park.' Such a sentence would be regarded as a structural *faux pas* by pedantic linguists and all those who insist on consistently correct relationships of the subject and object! (Even the grammar alert mechanism on my PC underlined this apparently 'mistaken' use of language.) The more friendly informality of the **noun** 'Smudge' hints at a different attitude to his child than the precision of the name 'Charles' suggests about the way the woman feels about her son (the boy is never 'Charlie' and certainly not 'Chuck'!). The man continues (about the dog):

He loves it there. I wish I had half the energy he's got.

This first short sentence highlights clearly and unambiguously the dog's pleasure, contrasting so strongly with the man's melancholy. The 'I wish' at the beginning of the second sentence points to that wistful comparison. And he uses a **contraction**, 'he's'! No such contractions appear in the whole of the woman's version of events, thus underscoring the direct contrast of the two adult characters.

The little boy's narrative has some of the same characteristics as the man's. He is also unhappy.

I was at home on my own again. It's so boring. Then Mummy said that it was time for our walk. There was a very friendly dog in the park and Victoria was having a great time. I wished I was.

The **adverbial phrase** 'on my own again' is very plaintive. This is immediately followed by 'It's so boring'; a most uncompromising commentary on his perception of the situation in which he has been placed. A few sentences later he makes another pointed comment in the same style: 'I wished I was.' These devices act in an almost choric manner, summarising for the reader how the character truly feels. They are entirely deliberate choices by the author to convey exactly how the reader should be interpreting this protagonist's perceptions. Certain words he utters also have a relationship with, and help to point more specifically to, the words spoken by other characters in this narrative. He refers to his mother by the **noun** 'Mummy', wholly in keeping with the way she addresses him as 'Charles', and contrasting fully with the way the man calls his daughter 'Smudge'; the girl, in turn, refers to her father as 'Dad'. (Readers will see, as they continue through each narrative, that the woman actually treats the dog better than her son!) The boy relates that his mother said 'it was time for our walk', thus echoing exactly her linguistic phrases and her values. His use of the **adjective** 'friendly', applied to the dog, contradicts directly his mother's sense of what is taking place, and juxtaposes with his own sense of loneliness.

When the little girl begins telling her story, everything else falls into place. She has a clear-sighted, positive attitude that manages to offer a realistic perspective to the versions of the other three.

> Dad had been really fed up, so I was pleased when he said we could take Albert to the park. Albert's always in such a hurry to be let off his lead. He went straight up to this lovely dog and sniffed its bum (he always does that). Of course, the other dog didn't mind, but its owner was really angry, the silly twit.

The **adverbial phrase** 'really fed up' (answering the question, 'how had he *been* feeling?') sums up immediately her father's mood, and leads to her own feeling (a **verb phrase**) 'was pleased', when she can do something about helping him. Albert, their dog, is a lively, happy animal, described as 'always in a hurry to be let off his lead'. The real contrast is to be discovered in the **compound sentence** 'He went straight up to this lovely dog and sniffed its bum (he always does that).' Readers will quickly notice the difference between the ways the First and Fourth Voices represent the meeting of the two dogs, through their different choice of **verbs** and the **objects** of those verbs: 'started bothering her' and 'sniffed its bum'!

The woman is seen to be using **euphemism** in her avoidance of an act she finds difficult to name, by substituting alternative 'polite' language. Further examples of the girl's attitude to her outing may be recognised in 'we both burst out laughing', and 'I felt really, really happy'.

This simple close study of language of a seemingly easy text is possibly one of the best preparations secondary pupils can enjoy in learning about how authors create character. Four different contrasting characters are established quickly and clearly in just a few words, and pupils are able to point to the obvious comparisons on which to base the evidence of their judgements. Even pupils with little linguistic confidence should be able to discern one type from another with real ease.

English teachers offering this sort of lesson to their classes do not need to emphasise the grammar as its focus. It is by no means essential to use technical terms for the grammatical instances being identified – but I think that such coyness would prevent pupils from being exposed to some important vocabulary that could be a valuable starting point for more advanced language knowledge. Teachers can encourage the straightforward comparisons of the characters as their starting point, and then tease out the linguistic features as they become more obvious, to illustrate how discovering and articulating further layers of meaning can make a relationship with a text more satisfying. Such exercises offer pupils more superior structured means to prise their way into texts than any number of 'comprehension' activities might offer. Throughout this book many other similar approaches will be suggested, to enable many young people in secondary schools to form a stronger relationship with the texts they are being asked to explain in their reading, or emulate in the writing contexts expected in school.

CHAPTER 1

'Grammar Wars': Grammar Teaching Since 1950

'Language has been treated as the compost heap in the walled garden of literature.' (Tim Shortis, NAAE Course, 1 July 2000)

Grammar teaching, 1945 to the 1960s

This is not intended to be a grammar book in the traditional way that such books were once understood. It offers a view about how useful the teaching of grammar, as a natural part of the English/literacy curriculum, can be in empowering secondary pupils in understanding and meaning-making in all their textual encounters. It contains some examples of how the employment of a reasonable knowledge of grammar enables teachers to offer their pupils a much broader repertoire of approaches in their endeavours to discover what texts are about, and how to make more deliberately structured and purposeful texts of their own. There are other much more focused and detailed books offering broader direct classroom application, to take forward the sorts of recommendations made in this one. They are listed at the back of the book.

The English strand of the Key Stage 3 Strategy, introduced to secondary schools in the summer of 2002, expects pupils to have more than a passing acquaintanceship with grammar, or 'sentence-level knowledge'. This requirement is the culmination of a movement to bring about the re-introduction of grammar teaching, certainly going back at least 30 years. Professor Brian Cox, chair of the committee responsible for the first English National Curriculum, writing in *The Times* in 1994 when a new crisis about teaching grammar was afflicting English teaching, stated:

Children need grammar and language to communicate effectively and make their way in society as individuals. This is English teaching's most basic function, but there is more. (Cox 1994)

He continues:

> The teaching methods in the 1930s relied heavily on rote learning and on boring exercises in parsing and clause analysis. . . In the 1950s and 1960s many good teachers started rejecting these old fashioned methods of teaching grammar because they were clearly not working. Research has shown again and again that mechanical exercises in grammar do not improve children's ability to communicate effectively.
>
> Unfortunately, in the 1960s, some teachers of English went to the other extreme. Because grammar had been taught badly, they taught no grammar. (*ibid.*)

Anyone attending an English lesson in most secondary schools soon after the Second World War could testify to this representation of the subject, embodied most clearly in the widespread adoption of a textbook series, *English Today*, first published by Ronald Ridout in 1947. He states his commitment to the value of grammar without equivocation, and his stance is quite clear in the following:

> The study of grammar helps us to understand the contribution each word, or group of words, has to make to the total meaning we wish to convey by our sentence. If we can understand the work each word or group of words does, we shall be able to express ourselves more accurately, and this in turn will help us think more accurately.
>
> This alone should make the study of grammar worthwhile. But in addition we must remember that 'correct' grammar is the written record of what educated people say and write. By learning it, we therefore help ourselves to speak and write in a way acceptable and intelligible to all educated people – and they are rapidly becoming the majority of the English people. (Ridout 1947)

The emphasis on the idea of individual words building up into sentences is worth noting in his explanation. This attitude will contrast directly with a completely different approach to language to be explored in more detail throughout this book. It is also necessary to notice the emphasis Ridout places on 'accuracy' or correctness. Such attention to this sort of 'accuracy' was, in turn, thought to bring about focused, precise thinking. Such claims will not be sustained in this book!

After the introduction, Ridout goes on to offer the following exercise:

> Not twenty yards from the window runs a honeysuckle hedge, and close to the top a pair of linnets had with great cunning built their nest and

hatched their little brood.
From the above sentence pick out:

1. the subject of the verb 'had ... built'
2. the object of the verb 'had ... built'
3. the subject of the verb 'runs'
4. a collective noun
5. a common noun
6. an abstract noun
7. a transitive verb
8. an intransitive verb
9. two adjectives and the nouns they qualify
10. two conjunctions and the parts of the sentence they join. (*ibid.*)

This was a way of working in English that was, I believe, called 'the naming of parts'! As a pupil in a grammar school in the 1950s, I recall most of my English lessons in the lower school being filled with such material. Ronald Carter, in his book outlining the findings of the LINC project, cites a similar but even worse example of a passage in an O level paper employed as late as 1961:

Leaving childhood behind, I soon lost this desire to possess a goldfish. It is difficult to persuade oneself that a goldfish is happy and as soon as we have begun to doubt that some poor creature enjoys living with us we can take no pleasure in its company.
Using a new line for each, select one example from the above passage of *each* of the following:

(i) an infinitive used as the direct object of a verb
(ii) an infinitive used in apposition to a pronoun
(iii) a gerund
(iv) a present participle
(v) a past participle
(vi) an adjective used predicatively (i.e. as a complement).
(Carter 1990)

This passage has been constructed, that is, brought into the world, solely for the purpose of offering an example of analysis! It has no other purpose except to be studied, containing, quite unrealistically, all the recognisable features waiting to be 'spotted' by keen-eyed grammar fans. Little wonder that the study of grammar came to have such a poor standing in English classrooms.
The prevailing learning principle that drives this sort of exercise is

explicitly stated by Ridout on page 9. It is based on the notion that learners of language can be given tiny 'building blocks' of the raw material – separate bits, such as nouns, prepositions and conjunctions – which will then be put together with other bits to construct whole texts. There is an assumption that 'meaning' resides in these separate parts, and if all those components are correctly put together, then the language user will have solved the problem and created something worthwhile and meaningful. A secure knowledge of grammar was also believed to be the prerequisite for writing correctly. The English language, so the reasoning went, was based on the same structures as Latin. In this particular view, language had fossilised into a set of clear rule-based principles and could be quickly divided into 'correct' or 'incorrect' categories. Any 'straying' from the 'correct' path was a sign of sloppy thinking and needed immediate correction. Infinitives could not be split and prepositions were never to end sentences!

'Transparent grammar', 1960 to 1985

Ridout held sway with huge numbers of English teachers until the mid-1960s (and, depressingly, continued to have an influence in some schools for much longer!) A supposedly more 'liberal' textbook series, O'Malley and Thompson's *English One to Five* was published in 1955, which also sold very well, but in most respects it echoed the tones of its immediate predecessor, as the opening to *English One* demonstrates:

'Well' said Mr. Johnson, 'How did you get on?'

'Not too badly,' said Jack.

'It was lovely,' said Jill. 'Several of our friends are still with us, in the same class. And the gym has horses and ropes and netball and a badminton court . . .'

'And you can hardly see into the lab windows for glass thingamebobs and whatdyecallits,' said Jack.

'Did you like the teachers?' asked Mrs. Johnson.

'Of course it's only the first day,' said Jack cautiously, 'but I think one or two of them are perfectly smashing.'

'*Smashing*. That sounds an odd word. Pass me the dictionary, please, Mother.' (O'Malley and Thompson 1955)

After more of this period piece recount of 'Jack and Jill's' day at school, including a justification for 'word study' and grammar, the book offers its first example of a grammar exercise on the topic of subjects and objects of sentences. And so it goes on. . . . (Imagine reading such a passage to a group of Year 7 pupils in a modern comprehensive classroom. It would, however, provide excellent material for demonstrating how much the language – and some of our fundamental attitudes to the family, school and language itself – has changed.)

Considerable numbers of English lessons at that time were based on classes working through such texts regularly and steadily, moving slavishly from exercise to exercise chronologically through each book, as if there were some magic formula to their order. The books were divided into sections, each with an introductory passage, focusing the pupils' attention on some (usually morally 'improving') topic. This passage would be followed by a number of exercises, requiring the pupils to answer comprehension questions, copy out sections of text into which they might be expected to add any missing words, or demonstrate their knowledge of grammar by parsing short paragraphs in the style of the Ridout example above (p. 9–10).

In 1963, two quite different textbooks were published that were to influence deeply the work and attitudes of English teachers at that time: *English Through Experience* by Rowe and Emmens, and *Reflections* by Clements, Dixon and Stratta. Both books were thematically organised, and *English Through Experience* dropped the repetitive language exercises, instead including work on improving punctuation in the context of pupils' own writing. *Reflections* was even more revolutionary, containing virtually no exercises, but including extracts from established authors arranged in sociologically determined categories (Old Age, Parents and Children, The Home, etc.) offered for the sheer pleasure of reading them! To a great extent, these books shaped the teaching of English for at least the next 20 years, and planned grammar teaching diminished gradually during that period. These books were contemporary with major movements to change the nature of teaching in English.

English teaching was influenced at various stages by progressive teaching methods. Teaching styles, derived from active learning through drama, migrated into English. During the 1960s and 1970s language and equality became a significant issue in English teaching for a brief period raising questions about the dominance of standard English. Educational psychology influenced thinking about language and learning in the 1960s and 1970s. This combination began to give rise to more consciously inclusive and exploratory language practices in English teaching. During this period the trans-Atlantic Dartmouth seminar (1967) took place (written up in John Dixon's *Growth through English* (1967)) and advocated creative writing and the use of literature for self-exploration and for exploring the world. (Peim 2000)

A commonly applied interview question fired at prospective candidates for English teaching posts at that time would typically be: 'How do you teach language skills to the pupils?', usually answered with the response, 'Through the teaching of literature.' But that vague mantra was rarely challenged or expected to be developed further, because nobody else had a better response.

By 1973 the teaching of grammar in many schools was surrounded by much uncertainty. The following was the opening of a chapter on 'Language Teaching' contained in a book published by the Assistant Masters Association called *The Teaching of English in Secondary Schools*:

> When we started planning this book, one of the first tasks we set ourselves was for each of us to write a short paper on his attitude to language-teaching. Then we studied and discussed what each of us had written; re-defined, clarified and modified our statements; and continued to exchange ideas more or less regularly until it was no longer possible to delay the writing of this chapter. You see, we were afraid of the chapter. We knew before we began that hardly any two teachers of English agree with one another about what, if anything, should constitute language-teaching in secondary schools. We knew that experts in linguistics, experts in curriculum-development, admissions tutors in higher education, employers and the general public all disagree with one another and with the teachers in the schools about the same thing. (Watkins 1973)

The chapter concludes that teaching traditional grammar will have no benefits, but there is residual evidence that teachers still feel the need to undertake 'exercises' of some kind. This 'close-up' of teacher thinking at the time was wholly typical of what was happening across the country.

Yet, contrary to some widely shared myths about the subject, grammar teaching did not disappear entirely. A book about English written in the mid-1970s illustrates an increasingly common view about the teaching of language at that time. In a section tellingly entitled 'English language – can it be taught? If so how?' the author writes:

> As we have seen, distinctions between language and literature persist in the deliberations of educationists, in spite of the passionate advocacy of a unitary approach from the progressive quarter. Producers of textbooks,

too, however contemporary in style, as often as not distinguish between 'language' work and other activities and so do those responsible for timetables. The practice of designating Tuesday period three as 'grammar', and Thursday period five as 'composition' is not a thing of the past as many would wish. (Saunders 1976)

What the author really objects to, however, is the paucity and sheer inadequacy of the grammar programme taught in most English classrooms at the time.

> The facts are that the grammar expounded in the majority of school course books is over simple as a description of the ways in which language works, and that anyway it is based upon false premises. Whereas modern linguistics attempts to build up models for describing and analysing language as it exists in its complex variety of contexts and uses, the traditional school grammar prescribes, stating rules of 'correctness' which have only to be learned to render the pupil literate.
> (*ibid.*)

The committee serving under Sir Alan Bullock was commissioned in 1972 by the then Secretary of State for Education Margaret Thatcher, among other things, to consider in relation to schools:

1. all aspects of teaching the use of English, including reading, writing and speech;
2. how present practice might be improved and the role that initial and in-service training might play

It confirmed, to a great extent, what Michael Saunders had suggested was indeed the broad picture. In its survey of English teaching in schools the Bullock committee found:

> The traditional view of language teaching was, and indeed in many schools still is, prescriptive. It identified a set of correct forms and prescribed that these should be taught. As they were mastered the pupil would become a more competent writer and aspire to a standard of 'correctness' that would serve him *(sic)* for all occasions. Such a prescriptive view of language was based on a comparison with classical Latin, and it also mistakenly assumed an unchanging quality in both grammatical rules and word meaning in English. In fact the view still prevails. (Bullock 1974)

After magisterially commenting on the teaching of language through time, the committee then recounts:

> In our visits to schools we found that the teaching of language through weekly exercises was still commonly to be found at all age levels, but particularly in the primary school... In our discussion with secondary English teachers we found a good deal of uncertainty about the teaching of language. Some regarded language improvement as a by-product of the talk, writing and literature which formed the core of their work; and they gave it no specific attention. Others set aside one period a week for it, usually working from a course book. A substantial number considered that the express teaching of prescriptive language forms had been discredited, but that nothing had been put in its place. They could no longer subscribe to the weekly period of exercises, but they felt uneasy because they were not giving language regular attention. It seems to us that this uncertainty is fairly widespread, and that what many teachers now require is a readiness to develop fresh approaches to the teaching of language. (*ibid.*)

These findings were a fair summary of what took place for more than 20 years. When I began teaching in 1970, there were still periodic attacks by individual teachers on the teaching of grammar, but they were not systematic. Every so often, the teachers in the English department in which I worked – and, I was regularly led to understand through regional meetings, similarly in other departments – would bemoan the pupils' inability to punctuate correctly, and we would teach clauses, or there would be worries about subject–verb agreement, and we would tackle verbs for a few lessons. Before the introduction of the Literacy Strategy, primary colleagues, most of whom were not English specialists, filled considerable numbers of lessons with grammar exercises, because they believed that such an approach was the way language might be learned and improved. Primary teachers were not the only promoters of decontextualised grammar work however. As an English Inspector in the 1990s it was still not unusual for me to observe pupils busily undertaking work from ruthlessly dedicated language books such as *A Basic Course in English* (Wright 1961), but by that time such teachers were by far the minority. Teachers were never quite sure why they included such activities in their work, but they expressed vague ideas that, at best, they might be contributing to language development; at worst, they would not be making pupils' English any worse!

There was also a significant political dimension to the teaching of language, which cannot be ignored. Teaching grammar tended to be undertaken most readily (and knowledgeably) by more 'traditional' teachers of English, most of whom had themselves received an education comprising a substantial classical background. It is a well-known fact that society changed dramatically during the 1960s. English teachers were changing too – the men notable for their long hair and developing unconventionality in classrooms that had been more used to male teachers wearing blazers or leather-patched sports jackets, and women in their long, flowery wraps, resisting the former twin-set style. Many of these teachers were challenging the orthodoxies that had governed the subject for so long, certainly since the end of the war. These teachers, increasingly the products of English degree courses based on literary studies with little language content, rejected the rule-governed grammar basis to language teaching, yet were unable to replace such knowledge with a worthwhile substitute. In this same period the grammar/secondary modern school split was being seriously questioned nationally and was soon to be gradually overturned in most areas of the country and replaced by comprehensive schools. The rituals of established examinations were also being scrutinised carefully; so, in some subjects of the curriculum, the O level – the examination which symbolised the tripartite system that had existed since 1945 – was being replaced by CSE syllabuses, written and assessed by teachers themselves. In English, there was a growing belief in pupils' 'creativity', moving the central focus of the work in the subject into the hands of the pupil writer.

Rather than dictating what pupils should write, and insisting on traditional, formulaic approaches, teachers were promoting work that grew out of increasing real-life stimulus and direct experience. They encouraged the pupils to build their written work in stages, through processes from plan to first draft and then to final realisation.

> A substantial shift occurred in the types of writing task being set, with young writers being encouraged to express their feelings in their writing and to write from personal experience. The work of Donald Graves in America reinforced this stress upon the authentic voice of the child and added to it by suggesting that unless children understood the processes of writing then it was impossible for them to have full ownership of the product. (Myhill 2001b)

Many teachers made claims for the primacy of the content of writing; statements such as 'it doesn't matter how it has been written as long as it's interesting with something to say' were not wholly a parody of their thinking. Teachers adopted Graves' term 'the authentic voice' of the pupil, and interpreted it to suggest that children were somehow programmed naturally to write without any support, or adult intervention. Indeed, teachers – it was claimed by the more extreme advocates of this approach – would be likely to corrupt, or at best stifle, this creative outpouring by offering anything approaching teaching. Specific attention given to teaching or addressing aspects of grammar in the classroom became akin to suggesting the return of child flogging in such a context!

The Bullock Report went as far as recommending that training courses for teachers should contain an element of language study, equivalent to 100 hours, but in reality the exact manner of that training was left ultimately to each institution. Even in those institutions where the recommendations were adopted, there were considerable variations in the actual courses, not always making the sort of impact originally intended. An increasingly disparate situation was allowed to develop, causing growing concern for traditionalists, who were often given regular columns in right-of-centre newspapers to express their views. Teachers detected a growing 'hard line' in government thinking, and particular appointments to government-sponsored agencies, such as the School Curriculum and Assessment Authority (SCAA), charged with advising ministers about issues of the curriculum, were being offered to those outside the teaching profession who represented views of English not in contemporary accord with classroom practice. But that takes us too far ahead in this narrative.

'Thatcherite grammar and the anomaly of LINC': the 1980s and 1990s

Margaret Thatcher's Conservative election victory in 1979 signalled a new approach to teaching grammar in secondary English lessons. Her government was very much committed to the idea of more formal classroom practice, and saw its reintroduction as one of the main planks of improving pupils' literacy standards, which were once again under attack. It seemed that the 'new breed' of English teachers had to be outflanked. The sort of thinking that was resulting in this changed attitude may be seen in the following extract:

> we've allowed so many standards to slip . . . teachers weren't bothering to teach kids to spell and to punctuate properly . . . if you allow standards to slip to the stage where good English is no better than bad English, where people turn up filthy . . . at school . . . all those things cause people to have no standards at all, and once you lose standards then there's no imperative to stay out of crime. (Norman Tebbit – then chairman of the Conservative Party – *Today*, Radio 4, 1985)

During its first period of office the Thatcher government made its earliest tentative steps towards laying down the foundations of an eventual National Curriculum by publishing a series of documents called *Curriculum Matters*, and number one in the series was *English from 5 to 16* (DES 1984). While these publications were conceived originally as consultative papers, Sir Keith Joseph, then Secretary of State for Education and Science, stated in the covering letter:

> We endorse, subject to consultations, HMI's approach to the aims and objectives of English teaching and commend the teaching styles, methods and approaches which they suggest. We intend, subject to the outcome of the consultative process which the paper initiates, and in consultation with those concerned within and outside the education service, to move towards a statement of aims and objectives for English teaching in schools which can serve as a basis for policy at national and local level. (DES 1984)

Most English teachers were outraged. Yet much of their anger was directed towards only small parts of the booklet, the majority of the contents being regarded as sensible and straightforward. But the really 'offensive' sections reopened discussions that had previously been avoided for a long time. One example was paragraph 3.8:

> There is much confusion over whether grammar should be explicitly taught. It has long been recognised that formal exercises in the analysis and classification of language contribute little or nothing to the ability to use it. One consequence of this, however, is that many pupils are taught nothing at all about how language works as a system, and consequently do not understand the nature of their mistakes or how to put them right. We suggest that if some attention is given to the examination and discussion of the structure of the language pupils speak, write, read, or listen to for real purposes, their awareness of its possibilities and pitfalls can be sharpened. In the course of this, it is reasonable that they should learn such grammatical terminology as is useful to them for the discussion of language. But what and how much terminology they should be taught at any given stage must depend on how much they can assimilate with understanding and apply to purposes they see to be meaningful and interesting. The least able at using language are the least likely to understand the terminology, let alone apply it in any useful way. (*ibid.*)

The reaction which this small section of the pamphlet provoked could not have been worse if the DES had suggested the return of transportation for stealing sheep.

So great was the clamour from English teachers, the press and many other groups about this set of recommendations concerning the teaching of the language that the DES felt obliged to publish a follow-up booklet, *English from 5 to 16 – The Responses to Curriculum Matters 1*. It was the only set of subject proposals to warrant an official rejoinder. The first paragraph of this document explains itself:

> 1. *English from 5 to 16* caused a great deal of interest both within and outside the teaching profession. Responses were seldom from individuals speaking for themselves – most were the results of considerable discussion, often by large groups... The document was clearly successful in promoting discussion. It seldom left readers indifferent; it prompted respondents to express matters of belief, principle and practice which were close to their hearts. (DES 1986)

The authors of the booklet go on to be much more specific about the issues that caused the most controversy:

Knowledge about language

37. Nothing divided the respondents more than the issue of knowledge about language. Colouring the whole debate were the experiences, recalled by many teachers, of exactly the old style of grammar analysis headlined by some press reports. Those sit firmly in the memories of the majority as being 'tedious and useless' and research findings were invoked to reinforce the point. What was not widely noticed, however, was that the original paper also explicitly excluded this line of approach. (*ibid.*)

So, having raised the phantom, the authors stepped aside from further controversy. But the genie was out of the bottle and a momentum, moving towards a position where grammar would eventually feature more explicitly in the English curriculum, began to build. At the beginning of 1987 the government appointed a committee under the chairmanship of Sir John Kingman, the Vice-Chancellor of Bristol University, a mathematician (something of a surprise to many, but given the political circumstances not wholly startling). The committee comprised broadcasters, writers and journalists, as well as academic linguists and teachers, to address the following terms of reference:

1. To recommend a model of the English language, whether spoken or written, which would;
   - serve as the basis of how teachers are trained to understand how the

   English language works;
   • inform professional discussion of all aspects of English teaching.
2. To recommend the principles which should guide teachers on how far
   and in what ways the model should be made explicit to pupils, to make
   them conscious of how language is used in a range of contexts.
3. To recommend what, in general terms, pupils need to know about how
   the English language works and in consequence what they should have
   been taught, and be expected to understand, on this score, at ages 7, 11
   and 16. (DES 1988)

This unequivocal commitment to reintroducing some features of explicit
language teaching seemed to be a redefinition of the subject – particularly
when the terms of reference were posited on the notion of a single 'model
of language'.

   However, contrary to the worst expectations of some sceptics, the
Kingman Committee came to the following surprisingly clear conclusion:

> Nor do we see it as part of our task to plead for a return to old-fashioned
> grammar teaching and learning by rote. We have been impressed by the
> evidence we have received that this gave an inadequate account of the
> English language by treating it virtually as a branch of Latin, and
> constructing a rigid prescriptive code rather than a dynamic description
> of language in use. It was also ineffective as a means of developing a
> command of English in all its manifestations. Equally, at the other
> extreme, we reject the belief that any notion of correct or incorrect use of
> language is an affront to personal liberty. We also reject the belief that
> knowing how to use terminology in which to speak of language is
> undesirable. Language is, as a matter of observable fact, plainly governed
> by a series of conventions related to the varying audiences, context and
> purposes of its use. Successful communication depends upon a
> recognition and accurate use of the rules and conventions. Command of
> these rules and conventions is more likely to increase the freedom of the
> individual than diminish it. (HMSO 1988)

This extremely authoritative statement became a defining moment in the
continuing discussion about the teaching of language in English. A
distinction (very familiar to academic linguists before this time, but less
familiar to most teachers, even though it was made specifically by the
Bullock committee) had been drawn between 'prescriptive' and
'descriptive' models of grammar, thus changing the manner in which the
specific teaching of language could be introduced to the English classroom.
'Knowledge of language' also became a concept gaining increasing support

from this time. But this set of conclusions was not what the government had hoped for, and Mrs Thatcher, supported by a large right-wing group in the Conservative Party, was determined this would not be the last word on the matter.

Having already set up the Kingman committee, the government, particularly the seemingly very busy Secretary of State for Education, Kenneth Baker, became increasingly impatient, and switched to a new tactic to impose further a centralised will over schools, by taking on the major task of introducing a National Curriculum. English was the first subject to be dealt with in legislation set out in the Education Reform Act in 1988. Almost immediately after the committee, headed by Sir John Kingman, which had been charged to 'recommend a model of the English language as a basis for teacher training and professional discussion, and to consider how far and in what ways that model should be made explicit to pupils at various stages of education' (Cox 1991) had published its recommendations, another Working Group was assembled to set up the national programme intended to be the blueprint for English teaching for the next decade.

Mr Baker, believing that he could fashion a grammar-centred curriculum to challenge all that he and his colleagues felt was wrong with English teaching, invited Professor Brian Cox, an English academic at Manchester University, to head this Working Group. Brian Cox and a colleague had been the chief editors of a set of articles entitled 'The Black Papers on Education', unpopular with most teachers of English, published in *The Quarterly Review* between 1969 and 1977, which questioned the way the subject was taught, and claimed that standards had fallen badly. Kenneth Baker was convinced that Brian Cox would steer his Group towards an explicitly stressed 'hard-line', grammar-based curriculum, but the research about its new chairman had not been sound:

> When I first met my working group I was astonished to discover that they were far more progressive in outlook than members of the Kingman Committee. The Kingman Committee included traditionalists of an older generation such as Peter Levi, professor of Poetry at Oxford, and Patrick Kavanagh, a poet whose conservative views were well known from his regular column in *The Spectator*. They were with difficulty persuaded by the linguists on the Committee, particularly the Secretary, Peter Gannon (an HMI), and Professor Gillian Brown, at the time professor of Applied Linguistics at the University of Essex, to accept a model of language in tune with modern ideas and needs of the contemporary school. (Cox 1991)

Yet again, the English programme in the proposed National Curriculum that emerged from this Group was not the one the Conservative government had so keenly wanted or anticipated.

The Cox Working Group used its deliberations to bring about a pause in the rather frantic and not always well-informed debate about what should be included in the English curriculum. Professor Henry Widdowson, a member of the Kingman committee, had been permitted to write a dissenting appendix in that committee's final Report, pointing to issues that needed far more intelligent and less hurried consideration:

> The rationale for the model ought clearly to carry conviction. But as it is presented in Chapter 2, for all the interesting points it raises, it is, I think, pitched at too general and uncritical a level. This, I think, is because it does not come to grips with the central question of how knowledge about language can be shown to be relevant to the educational aims of English as a school subject.
>
> Indeed what these educational aims should be, what English is on the curriculum *for*, is not really explored here with any rigour but simply asserted in very general (and traditional) terms. (HMSO 1988)

Cox's committee did not address these types of central question very deeply, but at least they spent some time attempting to redefine and describe the subject in its own times.

> If we look at the range of statements about English teaching in books written before our Report we see how broad the subject is. It includes, for example, language use, language study, literature, drama and media education; it ranges from the teaching of a skill like handwriting, through the development of the imagination and of competence in reading, writing, speaking and listening, to the academic study of the greatest literature in English. Such broadness poses problems, both for the identity of English as a distinctive school subject and for its relations with other subjects on the school curriculum. Another consideration is that English can seem at first glance rather different in primary and in secondary schools. Primary teachers normally teach English as part of the integrated curriculum, whereas in secondary schools it is more usually taught in timetabled slots by subject specialists. (Cox 1991)

Cox's pause in the proceedings, taking time to reassess what the subject very broadly called 'English' was about, was timely during that delicate and vulnerable period in the late 1980s. But it was unable to resolve the many problems facing practitioners, at all levels and in many contexts, and did not point to a direction or focus likely to outline the coherent shape of the future. In some senses this continuing dilemma may, in retrospect, be seen as inevitable. The issue of to what degree language teaching should be included in the school curriculum was only one of the many struggles and changing perspectives taking place in the subject at the time.

Equally powerful arguments were beginning to be heard at school level about new approaches to the teaching of literature, challenging an earlier innocence which held that the teacher – who was believed to hold the key to 'meaning' – instructed the pupils, and inducted them into the freemasonry of discovering those correct insights for themselves. For many years there had been continuing disputes, discussions and disagreements about the part played by such activities as drama and media studies in English. There were similar disagreements about the types of text believed to be suitable or appropriate for study in English lessons, particularly in those areas of the country admitting increasingly larger numbers of pupils from other cultures. A few teachers of English in London had experimented with and devised English lessons based on long-term role-play situations, signalling yet another challenge to the familiar patterns that had characterised the way the subject was taught. Some ten years after these upheavals, Rob Pope asked the following questions, still obviously unresolved:

> Should we, for instance, speak of the medium of our subject as 'the English Language (definite article, upper case and singular), 'varieties of English' (plural features of a single entity) or, more provocatively, 'englishes' (flatly lower case and plural)? When speaking of one of the major objects of study, should it be 'English Literature' or 'literatures in English? (There's a big difference.) And in either case we need to be sure whether we're talking about canonical and/or non-canonical texts – conventionally recognised 'classics of Eng. Lit.' or something else. Yet again, in still more challenging vein, perhaps we had better say our subject is 'writings, speeches, performances, films and other media partly in some variety of english'? (Pope 1998)

Cox and his committee attempted to engage with some of the issues of language teaching, but there was little time for sophisticated exploration given the political pressures for a particular view of the subject, and for the completion of the National Curriculum deliberations. There was to be no sympathy from the Department of Education, headed by Kenneth Baker, or sections of the right-leaning press, when the final committee Report did not insist on a 'Latinate grammar' model. Indeed, when the Report was actually published, the Secretary of State was so unhappy with its sections outlining its rationale and explanations that he called for it to be changed from its original order, to relegate their importance:

> There was some question about whether the Report should be published in its entirety, for Mr Baker and Mrs Rumbold (a Minister in the Education department) were worried that there were sections which the Prime Minister would not like. On the other hand, if they failed to publish the whole Report this would anger the teaching profession and provide the journalists with a sensational story. A compromise was agreed. They were reasonably satisfied with chapters 15 to 17, which included the attainment targets and programmes of study, and so . . . it was decided to print these first. (Cox 1991)

Professor Widdowson's fundamental and straightforward question, 'What is English in the curriculum for?' was, then and later, never given the proper time and attention it really deserved. The forces driving the Thatcher government had no need to ask that same question – they were *sure* of the answer. Indeed, the certainty of the government was summarised succinctly by John Marenbon, a Cambridge don in medieval studies, selected – for his right-wing views – to lead a working party on English curriculum review. He was appointed to this position as a result of having written a very influential pamphlet prior to the construction of the National Curriculum that contributed hugely to its eventual shape:

> Grammatical and literary failings among young people are evidence that, in most schools today, English is badly taught, and that it used to be taught better. . . This new orthodoxy finds little value in grammatical correctness and has no place for literature as a heritage. (Marenbon 1987)

Louise Poulson, Senior Lecturer in Education at Exeter University, who has charted those times, summed up that period when she wrote:

> From the early 1990s, Conservative politicians, and their advisers, pursued a narrow and dogmatic definition of standard English, grammar and literary heritage. One of the most important ways in which they did this was by determining or influencing the membership of key agencies responsible for the implementation of the National Curriculum and assessment.
>
> The influence of right-wing pressure groups and think-tanks on the shaping of the English Curriculum was strong. In an address to one of these groups, John Marks argued that the teaching of English had become the main ideological battleground in Britain for those who

wanted to politicise education in a left wing direction. However, the evidence suggested that the politicisation of education was in much less danger from those with ideological leanings to the left than from those with strong leanings to the far right. (Poulson 1998)

However, the Conservative ministers at the Department of Education and Science were to drop one further bombshell. The government had itself commissioned a national project entitled 'Language in the National Curriculum' (LINC) in 1989, under the leadership of Professor Ronald Carter of the University of Nottingham, to:

> produce materials and to conduct activities to support implementation of English in the National Curriculum in England and Wales in the light of the views of language outlined in the Kingman and Cox Reports on English language teaching and English 5-16 respectively (DES 1988, 1989). The LINC project was designed to operate from April 1989 until March 1992. (Carter 1990)

This was a most peculiar venture for the Conservative government to be undertaking at that time. It had commissioned and established a committee, apparently with the 'correct' membership, intended to reach the conclusion that a prescriptive model of English grammar should be taught in English lessons. The committee had somehow failed to reach the required conclusion, after paying attention to informed evidence from a large range of genuinely qualified linguists and others. Extraordinarily, having been thoroughly dismayed at the recommendations of that committee, the government then devised a project, to be led by a linguist, to draw on the outcomes of the Kingman committee. This new project was somehow expected to provide the sorts of material capable of enabling the prescriptive view of language teaching to prevail.

The project was funded generously by the government, making it possible for the appointment of a network of highly able and very knowledgeable Consortium Coordinators to share national development responsibility issues, and to disseminate their work with English advisers, teachers and academics across the country in regular group meetings. At last there seemed to be a properly thought-through enterprise, based on sound theoretical grounding in modern linguistics, staffed by knowledgeable and enthusiastic practitioners capable of exploring and advising on the most appropriate place and role of grammar in the school curriculum. Enormous energy was invested in classroom studies of language at work, and many pupils were drawn into exciting research capable of increasing dramatically their linguistic understanding. Many classroom teachers' perspectives of grammar and its potential in their work were completely transformed by the sorts of activity sponsored and encouraged by the project. Evidence of the quality of that work may be seen in publications such as *Looking into Language* (1992), edited by Richard Bain, Bernadette Fitzgerald and Mike Taylor.

Unfortunately, the seeds of its own destruction could be detected in Ron Carter's introduction to the *LINC Reader*, quoting the research of Michael Halliday, on which the LINC project was posited:

> Particularly in a language education perspective, we need to take a dynamic view of language in all three dimensions of its variation; 'dialectal' (regional/social), 'diatypic' (functional) and 'diachronic' (historical). To put this in less technical terms: for any theory of language in education, it should be seen as the norm, rather than the exception, that the community of learners use a variety of codes (languages and/or dialects), that they use a variety of language functions (or registers), and that none of these ever stands still. (Halliday 1987, in Carter 1990)

These would not have been comfortable statements or have made much sense for politicians, who themselves had only the sketchiest knowledge of grammar. What little sense they made of the whole topic was to regard it as one of the immutable cornerstones of tradition in which they had invested so much. The notion that grammatical study was able to describe 'changes' in language was complete anathema to those who saw the reintroduction of a specific grammar curriculum as representing the best aspects of a former glorious age, and was destined to be the focus for the future. The complications of grammar suggested by Carter's well-intentioned explanation, and the mystifying language of terms such as 'dialectal', 'diatypic' and 'diachronic', were bound to alert junior ministers, carrying out the grand designs of their Cabinet superiors, to be at least suspicious of the LINC programme. Thus it proved to be.

Once again, Conservative dogma was to be disappointed. The LINC project failed increasingly to live up to ministerial expectations. As more of its work and knowledge of its areas of interest became available, the government and its 'advisers' grew increasingly alarmed. Reports suggested that pupils in school were to be asked to follow the recommendations of this project and to give serious thought, for instance, to the lyrics of popular music, and – even worse in the eyes of the paymasters – to study political documents, to understand better the language of power. The government could not undo the LINC project's work or proscribe its findings, but it could still restrict the effect it might have on schools. Therefore, a decision was made centrally not to publish the project's work, and teachers would find it difficult to access the materials. The networks that had been established for the dissemination of the research were no longer funded, and the contracts of the Consortium Coordinators were not extended.

In retrospect, this curmudgeonly set of attitudes may be seen to have been a massive act of academic vandalism. The government, at that moment, had the capability of bringing about a hugely informed teacher training programme, with the potential for widening the knowledge base of teachers in primary and secondary schools, but its entrenched simplistic monolithic view of language teaching and learning could not accept that a more subtle, intelligent interpretation had to be embraced. In a series of vitriolic and often misinformed newspaper and magazine articles, writers who were supportive of the government poured considerable bile on the project through June and July 1991 (Richmond 1992), justifying its premature closure. Meanwhile, teachers, English advisers and those close to the project were busy surreptitiously photocopying anything they could salvage, in the full knowledge that that particular official channel was closed.

It should be recognised that not every English teacher mourned the passing of the LINC project. Many had not been acquainted sufficiently with its possibilities in the first place and therefore had no idea of what had been lost. Some teachers were very suspicious of the ways in which the teaching of grammar as a result of this project may have been affected; they had the gravest worries about perceived requirements to teach and assess 'correct English', or Standard English, in writing and speaking. Articles appeared in professional publications and speakers addressed meetings of English teachers about fears of assessment being closely tied to limited examples of children's knowledge of grammar. The 'model' of grammar produced by the Kingman committee was also not easily understood by a generation of English teachers who had themselves not been taught much about the topic in their own education. Many were limited to seeing classroom studies based on grammar merely as ways of serving notions of 'correctness', and had little idea of its new potential.

> One area of language study in which there was rather less agreement and with which there was some discomfort, was the teaching and learning of language structure and forms. There was little, if any, reference to the direct teaching of the forms and structure of language; the only context in which this aspect of language teaching was mentioned was in reference to proposals to include greater emphasis on grammar and standard English in the statutory National Curriculum for schools. . . Systematic and explicit study of language structure would necessitate a shift away

from normative ideas held by teachers about the subject. In particular, it would necessitate a change of attitudes and beliefs of English teachers about the nature and place of language study in the curriculum and their own conceptions of language as a body of knowledge. (Poulson 1998)

The introduction of the National Curriculum in English in the early 1990s in no way concluded or resolved the problems of teaching grammar in the curriculum. In fact, it signalled the beginning of the most contentious period in the differences between the Department of Education (with its legion of politically motivated advisers) and practising teachers. The ink had barely dried on the original curriculum programme, as recommended by the Cox committee, before the government introduced machinery to 'review' and change the published programme. The political influences, recognised most easily in a pressure group called the Centre for Policy Studies (CPS), continued to have an effect completely out of proportion to their size and educational knowledge. John Marenbon, a notable figure in the CPS, wrote a badly misinformed pamphlet *English Our English* in 1987, denying that grammar had a 'descriptive' function, claiming that Standard English is 'superior' to dialect and insisting that teachers of English:

recognise English as a subject – no more and no less: the subject in which pupils learn to write standard English correctly and thereby to speak it well, and in which they become acquainted with some of the English literary heritage. (Marenbon 1987)

These views, from a Cambridge academic whose total teaching experience had to do with a tiny core of highly articulate undergraduates in a very specialised area of study, had little resonance with teachers of English across the country. In metropolitan centres such as London and Leeds, many English teachers who worked every day alongside children from a huge range of social classes, and – in some extreme cases – from as many as 50 different language backgrounds, felt that their teaching contexts were simply not understood. Government ministers, themselves taught largely in small classes in very traditional ways at expensive public schools, had absolutely no idea what the reality of language learning was for the majority of pupils in most maintained schools. Yet it was the CPS pamphlet that shaped the direction of the English curriculum until the Conservative government was itself ousted by New Labour in 1997.

In 1992, the new Secretary of State for Education, John Patten, had replaced the chairman of the National Curriculum Council (NCC), a former Chief Education Officer with huge experience of all aspects of education, with a former oil company executive, who had worked in Mrs Thatcher's policy unit at 10 Downing Street – connected with the CPS! It was the clearest signal that 'insider' professional advice would no longer be heeded in educational policy. Having experienced only three years of a National Curriculum that most teachers agreed was working well and becoming successfully embedded, the Secretary of State announced that the English programme would be reviewed. The new NCC chairman, David Pascall, published the document *National Curriculum English: The Case for Revising the Order*, purportedly based on a 'range of evidence' (never specified), suggesting:

> We consider, however, that the knowledge and skills involved in speaking, reading and writing need to be defined more explicitly and rigorously. In addition, the Order should provide a clearly defined and balanced framework in which pupils are taught to read, are encouraged to read widely, and are introduced to the excitement of great literature. Our proposals would result in three attainment targets – speaking and listening; reading including literature; and writing including spelling, grammar and handwriting. (NCC 1992)

This review – with its unambiguous attention to details of 'great literature' and 'grammar' – was to take away teachers' rights to choose the texts they could employ in their classrooms, and to introduce assessment procedures ensuring that the 'great literature' would be taught. Yet, in the long run, grammar was not the main issue to emerge from the complicated procedures that eventually saw the resignation of Pascall, to be replaced by Sir Ron Dearing.

But grammar was not dead as an issue, merely sleeping. The 'hard-line' approach favoured by right-wing ideologues was displaced from centre stage for a short period, for a number of reasons. Teachers of English had become 'distracted' momentarily by the prospect of being required to teach texts from specified historical periods, and some fierce disputes raging around the country about the structuring of the proposed Key Stage 3 tests. For a couple of years they devoted most of their time to resisting possibly the silliest document ever to be foisted on the profession; an anthology of unrelated, many quite unengaging and irrelevant, textual extracts and poems.

Yet many teachers continued to be bothered about their pupils' lack of specific language knowledge, and, from all the wranglings, disagreements and political posturings of the late 1980s and early 1990s, it was clear that only the most limited progress had been made. Much heat had been generated, but little light shed. Two practising teachers, Jane Lodge and

Paul Evans, wrote a chapter (interestingly called 'How do we teach grammar?' indicating, on the one hand, that the matter was still to be resolved, but, on the other, it could be approached only through the form of a plaintive question) in a significant book of that period, beginning:

> The subject of 'grammar' is a controversial one. There seems to be no general agreement even about what it is, which is the reason why we shall confine the word within inverted commas until we have defined it, at least to our own satisfaction. (Lodge and Evans 1995)

This situation was no more advanced than the discomfort expressed in the book published by the Assistant Masters Association 20 years before. They offered the following advice to the question in their title:

> Our answer is: Hold true to your own philosophy of teaching, be absolutely clear about your objectives and strategies and always keep yourself informed and open to change. (*ibid.*)

Hardly the most illuminating position! In fairness, they did go on to recommend that teachers should draw on pupils' intrinsic language knowledge, that grammar should be 'explored' and not taught, and that tentatively moving towards a position of making pupils aware of the way grammar contributes to knowledge of form of text could benefit both pupils' construction and analysis of text. It was not surprising then, that if, after all the years in which this 'controversial' topic was being considered by teachers they were no further forward in their thinking than these vague suggestions, other, more opinionated and confident voices would be ready to fill the spaces of their indecision.

'Repositioning and restoring grammar': the late 1990s to the present day

Geoff Barton, a prolific writer about English issues in the 1990s, always based on a personal, experienced, solid classroom perspective, was more candid and direct than the writers previously quoted in this chapter. In an address to the English Association in October 1997, subsequently reprinted in *The Use of English* magazine, he made the following honest case:

> The scandal of late 20th century English teaching is that if we asked most of our students what they thought about grammar, they wouldn't know the meaning of the word.

> I believe we've lost our way as English teachers, and certainly lost confidence about what grammar is – whether we should formally teach it and, if so, how.
>
> So, at best we tinker with it, photocopying the odd page of a coursebook from the stockcupboard. We have a quick blitz on nouns or full stops, or reassure by dishing out activities designed chiefly to amuse and entertain. Our nervous message to our students is 'you see, this isn't so bad is it?' and we make ourselves feel better for having 'done grammar'.
>
> Or perhaps we ignore it – as I did largely for the first five years of my teaching.
>
> Or we make our students jump like confused little dogs through hoop after hoop of meaningless exercises.
>
> Or – worst of all – we say we teach it in context, and thereby leave a child's experience of formal grammar teaching to total chance. If I happen to notice something they need to know, I teach it: if I don't it's left untaught. (Barton 1998)

This article, unlike many others beginning in the same descriptive manner, actually goes on to offer a possible model for progression, and shows itself ready to deal with, and familiarise pupils with, some of the technical language contributing to sentence-level knowledge. Yet it is worth comparing this quotation with the findings of the Bullock committee, quoted on page 15. If Barton's analysis of this situation was in any way accurate (and I believe there was good evidence to suggest that it was), it would appear that virtually no change had been effected about teaching grammar for a quarter of a century! Despite the nods to initiatives such as 'knowledge about language' and the huff and puff by traditionalists, English teachers were fairly certain about what they *did not* want to teach, but they had established almost no consensus about what they *did* want their pupils to know, or how that teaching ought to be conducted.

Curiously, the teaching of grammar was thriving in one area of English studies during this period. From the early 1990s a quiet revolution was taking shape in many sixth forms. The English A level language paper was becoming increasingly attractive in many schools, for a number of understandable reasons. Schools implementing this programme reported that the language paper seemed to be more attractive to boys than its literature equivalent, and that the teachers who were learning to teach it had been enormously excited by the new light it shed on the texts being studied. These teachers also discovered that by finding out more about language for their direct teaching needs, they experienced fresh insight in much of the rest of their work. Barbara Bleiman, writing in *The English and Media Magazine* in 1999 about her own introduction to teaching language for the first time at A level, shared the following:

> When I started teaching Language and Literature A Level recently, I knew that I had a lot of homework to do. It's one thing offering the occasional off-the-cuff definition of nouns or verbs, explaining where a full stop should go or suggesting that a sentence be broken down into shorter segments. It's quite another knowing that you have to explicitly teach a complete framework for the study of language. (Bleiman 1999)

She goes on, very positively:

> as an English teacher stepping into a different area of English studies, Linguistics was for me both threatening in its complexity and difference but also exciting in the possibilities it offered for the kind of discipline and rigour that had proved elusive within the literary tradition. (*ibid.*)

Then, in 1998, after a period of relative quiet in respect of teaching grammar, a number of separate developments once again forced teachers of English to reconsider the topic. First, QCA (the Qualifications and Curriculum Authority, a replacement for the former SCAA) refocused the attention of English teachers by publishing *The Grammar Papers – Perspectives on the Teaching of Grammar in the National Curriculum*. The Introduction to this document summarised a situation already explored in some detail in this chapter:

> Since the introduction of the revised English order in 1995 there has been much debate about the teaching of grammar. Evidence from the monitoring programme carried out by the School Curriculum and Assessment Authority (SCAA) in 1995–7 showed there is widespread uncertainty as to how to interpret and implement the grammar requirements in the national curriculum. Discussion with teachers indicated that there is little consensus about:
>
> - the role of grammar in the English curriculum;
> - how to integrate the teaching of grammar within the overall programme for English;
> - the nature and extent of grammatical knowledge needed by teachers;
> - whether pupils' grammatical knowledge needs to be explicit;
> - how pupils' grammatical knowledge and understanding can be assessed.

The issues were not in doubt, but this particular document was not likely to offer English teachers the sort of lead and direction so many of them wanted. It was not a well-structured booklet, devoting disproportionate space to the aspects of grammar unfamiliar to most teachers in a manner not designed to make them more interested in the topic. It had no guiding view or suggested approach to grammar – perpetuating the vacuum that had existed in the centre of the language-based curriculum for at least 25 years. The separate 'papers' were not organised coherently. Worst of all, it was accompanied by a most formidable draft assessment paper that failed to follow through the approaches recommended in the actual document. Quite rightly, *The Grammar Papers* encouraged grammar teaching that should:

- involve teacher exposition;
- encourage pupil investigation;
- focus on individual pupils' needs;
- refer to previous grammar teaching;
- include responses to, and assessment of, pupils' oral and written work.

Yet the draft 'test' paper reminded teachers of the types of language assessment paper administered 30 years previously; not quite involving the full parsing exercises of those times, but resembling them closely. The test exercises failed to reflect the suggested 'teaching' styles quoted above, requiring pupils to demonstrate language knowledge that was not contained in real contexts. While the document contained a valuable update of recent research pertaining to successful grammar teaching, this was not the sort of information most classroom teachers were seeking, and this particular booklet was quickly shelved in most English departments, not to be opened again.

A further significant development caused yet another burst of interest in the topic of teaching language in English. In the summer of 1998 the National Literacy Strategy was introduced to the vast majority of primary schools in England. Contained prominently within this programme was an explicit requirement that pupils aged from 5 to 11 would be taught 'sentence-level' knowledge, a phrase that really meant 'grammar knowledge'. Not surprisingly in its earliest stages, huge numbers of primary teachers were frightened by the prospect of teaching grammar – which few had experienced in their own schooling and teacher training – and this area of strategy remained temporarily undeveloped. But the classroom emphasis on, for instance, non-fiction 'text types' began to offer a pathway for the closer exploration of language through reading, and as a supporting structure for pupils' writing. One of the major problems for teachers in the earliest stages of the Strategy was the difficulty of finding suitable materials for classroom study. Inevitably, the educational publishing business rushed into print with collections of 'reductionist' grammar textbooks and pointless, time-filling worksheets, too readily adopted in some schools. Happily, many adventurous teachers began to explore real texts in closely analytical ways with their pupils, bringing about valuable language learning well beyond the mere 'naming of parts'. Anecdotal evidence from secondary schools in all parts of the country soon suggested that pupils who had experienced the best interpretations of this programme were arriving in Year 7 with more valuable insights about how language was at work in their classroom-based texts. Where primary schools had been encouraged to take the lead, secondary English teachers would soon be expected to follow and develop.

In 1999, QCA published two further documents intended to contribute to the growing trend of moving considerations about grammar into the mainstream of English teaching. *Not Whether But How – Teaching Grammar in English at Key Stages 3 and 4*, claimed to reflect:

> the changing debate and addresses concerns about how best to teach grammar. It explores the implications of the principles set out in *The grammar papers* and gives examples of how the principles can be put into practice. It offers further guidance on the teaching of grammar at key stages 3 and 4, but does not attempt to provide complete answers in an area where much needs to be developed. (QCA 1999a)

This booklet was much more reflective, offering a more genuinely exploratory attitude than its predecessor of less than a year before, and contained some good examples of practical approaches in classrooms. Unfortunately, appearing so soon after *The Grammar Papers,* it suffered by not receiving anything like the attention it deserved. Given the short space of time between the production of the two papers, the second one is actually a very different and much more helpful publication, and deserves wider support and follow-up. The other QCA document of that year, germane to this history, was *Improving Writing at Key Stages 3 and 4*. This booklet was the outcome and summary of a project begun in 1996, designed to 'investigate the accuracy and effectiveness of pupils' writing in GCSE examinations'.

> The Technical Accuracy Project looked at whole pieces of writing for textual organisation and paragraphing, and a 100-word block of text was used for the analysis of spelling, punctuation, word class usage, sentence and clause structure, and non-standard English. Furthermore the coding frames made a distinction between narrative and non-narrative texts.

This methodology allowed comparisons about features of writing to be made between different text types, between coursework and examination writing, between boys and girls and across grades. (QCA 1999b)

For the first time, English teachers were able to see a detailed linguistic analysis of their pupils' work and to have explained for them the sorts of characteristics likely to indicate whether a writer would be placed at a particular writing assessment National Curriculum 'level'. This development was welcomed in many schools, and teachers were pleased that a further dimension had been added to support their classroom practices.

> The data produced a complex picture of pupils' writing and has enabled the description in linguistic terms of features that are often part of impression marking but are not well articulated. When we talk of the qualities of an effective piece of writing, either among teachers or to pupils in the classroom how is that effectiveness described? This study roots such discussion in more specific terms, such as the effectiveness of openings or closure, the way the reader-writer relationship is established, or the coherence of the piece. (*ibid.*)

Many of the findings of this study will be referred to in greater detail in the chapter exploring how grammar knowledge can improve writing. A few findings, however, immediately made an impact on English teachers hoping to offer the sort of teaching and advice designed to bring about significant improvement in their pupils' work. One very noticeable comparison that can be made between the writing of A grade candidates and those achieving C and F grades is to be found in their use of verbs. A grade writers use few finite verbs, adding narrative detail through the use of 'adverbials', 'premodification' and non-finite participial clauses. The writing of F grade candidates, however, is driven almost entirely by its verbs, with little colouring from adjectival and adverbial details. An awareness of these features offers teachers a basis on which to plan and organise lessons designed to address these problems, as ways of attempting to improve the work of all pupils.

However, there were detractors:

> Where my reservations about approaching writing through this kind of limited linguistic analysis have been intensified, all QCA's earlier uncertainties about the value of an explicitly grammatical approach appear to have vanished altogether. They inform us that some of the features

identified by the TAP (Technical Accuracy Project) analysis 'clearly require more systematic teaching'. These include *clause structure* and *patterns of word class usage*. 'To ensure that these aspects receive specific attention, it is necessary to plan explicitly for their coverage.' (D'Arcy n.d.)

Notice that hiss of in-drawn breath at the thought of pupils being taught about 'clause structure' and 'patterns of word class usage'! At least 30 years after this debate began in earnest the spectre of 'prescriptivism' still hangs over the questions about grammar teaching like a dark shadow. The belief that pupils having to learn the specific terms of linguistic metalangue will, in that very act, be prevented from writing any further in their 'authentic voice' is still very potent with some teachers.

Yet the National Literacy Strategy, in its manifestations in three key stages, has demonstrated a clear shift in the way central government legislates for language growth and understanding. This same changing attitude seems to be echoed by QCA, as Chris Davies has observed recently:

> A number of efforts are also coming currently from QCA to establish a meaningful kind of grammar teaching at secondary level. It does not appear to be the intention here, either to prescribe correct language behaviour so much as to introduce the technical understandings about sentence construction and the composition of whole texts, that are potentially as much implied by the word 'grammar' as the more rigid notions of correctness that the word traditionally represents to the outside world. In effect, in the same spirit of the National Literacy Strategy, the hope is that a more intensive effort to provide children with a varied technical language about the workings of language will result – among other things – in a population of more accurate, flexible and autonomous language users. Whether or not this will prove to be the case only time will tell, but the spirit of these attempts is considerably more ambitious and far-reaching than anything advocated by the traditionalists from outside the profession. (Davies 2000)

The position of language or grammar teaching in the English curriculum has been a difficult one, leading sometimes to acrimony and great disagreement. Everybody is quite clear that teaching 'parts of speech' and just learning the terms is not likely to lead to real learning of language, or improvement of or further insight into linguistic texts. But there has been little consideration of a balanced, integrated approach of grammar (or language) knowledge that requires pupils to pay more attention to linguistic features within broad ideas of genre outlines. Writing situations where they have a purposeful sense of what they are trying to achieve, because they *want* to write, but can be taught to look into *how* they are writing with greater attention rarely seems to have been covered in the academic articles on the subject. Quite simply, the case for teaching any form of grammar in English lessons is not fully proven in either direction. Colin Harrison, in his recent study of research for the Key Stage 3 Strategy (Harrison 2002), states the following:

> Policy makers may well believe strongly that since good writing is grammatically accurate, and uses appropriately a rich variety of grammatical structures, it is essential that grammar should be taught, and taught early. But there is one problem if what is looked for is evidence-based policy: this is that 'research reviews have consistently failed to provide evidence that grammar teaching makes any difference to the quality of pupils' writing.' (Harrison 2002)

Mary Hilton, actually making a case for not adopting the 'rigid objectives-led' programme set out by the NLS in primary classrooms, and insisting that teachers in that phase should 'recapitulate the essentials of strong primary practice with regard to writing', states:

> The aim is *not* to impart knowledge about language but to develop each child's individual writing voice. Having something to say – and knowing whatever it is will be valued by the reader – is the first step to effective communication in writing. (Hilton 2001)

But the methods Hilton is referring to have not improved writing during the last decade – so the central educational administrators would claim – and something different has to be explored. But, that 'something different' does not necessarily mean returning to those unsuccessful tactics relying on children being subjected to grammatical 'driller, killer' approaches, so discredited years ago, which appears to be the only alternative that those educational professionals who fear for the loss of creative skills seem to claim.

Tony Burgess, in a talk to a NATE day conference in June 2001, published in the series 'Perspectives on English Teaching' in a book called *'When the Hurly Burly's Done': What's Worth Fighting for in English Education?* offers a balanced perspective and suggests that integration must be the way forward:

> LINC's model is essentially the Hallidayan model, it is the model of Norman Fairclough, and the model of critical linguists. In essential

orientation, this is the model of the new secondary English framework, which seeks to build from the teaching of forms, through textual study, towards a critical approach to texts. At the risk of oversimplifying the intentions, it is possible to see a central contrast. In all the Britton work, and in the subsequent American work on process, the focus is on the person using the language, on the learner, on the writer. In the anthropological tradition the focus is similarly on the person, learning differential literacies. Texts figure, but are subordinate to a wider developmental perspective. In the model from the new linguistics, the focus is on text. You do not exclude these other traditions by such a focus, but you begin to implement a further hierarchy of considerations for pedagogy, and this is where the room is needed for discussion and for the creativity of practice to breathe.

The right approach is surely synthesis. It is not impossible to conceive a practice that attends to the kinds of modelling and to the more explicit forms of instruction that are proposed through concentrating on text, but does not neglect attention to the writer or to wider cultural considerations concerning literacy. (Burgess 2001; emphasis added)

The proposals and suggestions that follow in this book are posited from that same conclusion. The grammatical or language knowledge stance of the book recognises that the Key Stage 3 *Framework* is a reality, but it cannot be properly effective unless teachers of English have decided, in the first place, on a view of language learning, and have put in place agreed and clear ideas about what constitutes 'good' writers. The strategy offers an entitlement teaching overview: teachers of English have to bring those teaching practices into play in a learning context that will be decided outside the aegis of the Strategy.

CHAPTER 2

What Sort of Grammar Study Could Improve Language Use?

> Bringing grammar to life is not a matter for classroom gimmicks to inject a few E numbers into otherwise mechanical lessons on adjectives, prefixes, collective nouns or whatever. It is a matter of recognising that grammar is not just a box of labels in a dissection laboratory but a living force used every moment words are uttered. (Keith 1997)

Very simply: grammar is everywhere and all of the time. One of the major tasks of English teachers is to enable pupils of all ages, abilities and attainment to 'notice' (i.e. really pay attention to the fact) that grammar is not a commodity that is turned on and off in certain lessons or learning contexts, but actually *is* all the lessons – and all the other encounters – in which they constantly engage. The most troublesome problem with language is that from the moment we are born it is always surrounding us. We fail to notice it – much like the air we breathe – because it becomes the material of our social relationships, our own thinking and learning, and our overall intellectual development. We never have to search for it or make it happen, and, unless someone who is more aware of its presence than ourselves makes us pay real attention to it, we continue to use it without having any noticeable cognisance.

> Thus as we use our own language, we inevitably use the grammar. We may not be able to describe it or talk about it, but we use it. We know the grammar implicitly, as people acknowledge when they say they have a feel for language or an idea of what 'sounds right'. (Collerson 1997)

Our language is not an isolated, stand-alone system of words or ideas. It is wholly of our culture, and central to the whole way of life we construct for ourselves. Language is the material for the ways of forming our many and various relationships with each other, and at any one moment its organisation offers clues to the manner in which those relationships and interactions are being conducted.

Whether or not they are aware of it, children – and all other language users of any degree – are constantly learning language, learning through language and learning about language. Teachers who want their pupils to pay greater purposeful attention to this immense area of what it means to be a social animal face a massive strategic problem. On the one hand, they have to successfully sense and outline the size of the overall picture of language, while, on the other hand, they have to select the worthwhile, individual features of it for classroom study and exploration that might contribute to their pupils using their new insights in myriad useful ways.

To enable them to be fully comfortable and confident in this area of very contrasting scales of size, teachers need to have established for themselves a workable and valid view of grammar that they can, in turn, share explicitly with their pupils. Otherwise, no real progress in language learning will have been made since the days of those lessons described in the Bullock Report in the early 1970s, or as described by Geoff Barton in Chapter 1 (pp. 30–1), when 'scraps' of language were served up to pupils in no systematic way as particular, unrelated 'needs' made themselves evident. Some English teachers have been impatient with or reluctant to address 'theory' (usually dismissed in a slightly sneering tone by its detractors) in their work in the past, but this state of affairs will have to change in the future if pupils are to be situated more firmly and successfully in their own learning processes.

> Theory – as a kind of technology for thinking – is vitally important in motivating significant transformations of the subject for student teachers and for qualified teachers. The term 'theory' signifies ideas that address the fundamental business of the subject – language, textuality and identity – and enable us to explore more explicitly the relations between these things and the social dimension of education. Current discourses of school improvement, professional proficiency and competence fail to address questions in this area of the cultural politics of English teaching. It is important for English teachers to be involved in a revival of professional debate about subject identity and the governance of English. (Peim 2000)

Recent researchers into learning (Black and Wiliam 1998; Clarke 2001) have shown teachers that, if they want them to learn, they must make absolutely clear to their pupils what they want them to learn. The corollary of this position, however, is that teachers must have a well-informed knowledge of what their pupils already know, to ensure that new learning is well founded. Young people in English classrooms, as in all other subjects of the curriculum, will not make sufficient progress unless they are able to articulate clearly for themselves the characteristics of those learning areas in which they are expected to make progress.

Unfortunately, English teachers at Key Stage 3 will not find the National Literacy Strategy very helpful as they position themselves relative to different views of language teaching and learning. The Strategy certainly requires teachers to address issues of 'sentence-level' knowledge more explicitly, but it fails to offer any sort of guidance or map to outline the notional shape and ultimate development of such knowledge. When secondary teachers realised that the Key Stage 3 Strategy would expect them to teach more specific language-based lessons, extending the same issues and strands contained in the primary strategy, there was an understandable nervous reaction from those who realised that their own skills had been developed insufficiently as pupils in their own right, or through teacher training. Yet, however hard they search, teachers – however knowledgeable – will find no help on this matter by consulting the *KS 3 Framework* (DfEE 2001) document, beyond the summary that 'sentence-level' work comprises:

- sentence construction and punctuation
- paragraphing and cohesion
- stylistic conventions
- standard English and language variation (DfEE 2001, p. 11)

and the advice that 'planning should draw together objectives from Word, Sentence and Text level'.

The *Year 7 Sentence Level Bank* (DfEE 2001a) helpfully provided by the National Literacy Strategy team will offer no further ideas or guidance about the nature of the grammatical ideas and knowledge likely to be of benefit to pupils in their English/literacy encounters. There is a huge difference between the 'why should I bother with this focus?' philosophical and pedagogical approach, and 'these are the sorts of exercises you might try with your classes', and the *Sentence Level Bank* tends towards the latter approach. No serious view of what might possibly be achieved through giving specific attention to grammar teaching and learning has been supplied, but lots of exercises are offered. The Introduction merely gives the following explanation:

> The focus is on using the sentence level objectives in the context of shared writing. Care has been taken to explore sentence construction in reading, and to demonstrate the conventions of sentence level grammar. These are then carried forward into the context of writing, when other skills and considerations are in play. The emphasis is on putting

knowledge about language to use, rather than treating it in isolation. (DfEE 2001a)

So we learn from this passage that:

- reading and writing are connected;
- writing comes about through a number of simultaneous processes;
- grammar should not be undertaken in a decontextualised manner.

These are are all extremely laudable snippets of information in themselves, but there is no exploration of what sort of grammar is being referred to in this circumstance. The booklet then goes on to provide 40 pages of 'contextual' Objectives, such as Objective S1 3, 'Using subordinate clauses'. The booklet informs its audience:

- Complex sentences link ideas together. They contain main and subordinate clauses. A main clause is one that is self-contained, that can act as a free-standing sentence. The subordinate clauses cannot make sense alone. In fact, Americans call the subordinate clause the *dependent* clause. It is very often heralded by a conjunction which suggests its dependent *status* (e.g. despite, although). (*ibid.*, p. 6)

Not once, however, is there to be found among these sorts of assertions any sort of explanation about why writers – of whatever status – might want to employ complex sentences. If writers intend a clear, unobstructed pathway to the meaning-making processes of their readers, it would be reasonable to assume that straightforward, unadorned, unequivocal methods of making contact would be the most efficient way of conveying what is being shared. So, why should 'complex sentences' need to be employed in preference to 'simple sentences'? But these matters are not considered.

This same criticism may also be applied to the section on the next page of the *Sentence Level Bank* (p. 7) headed 'To apply this objective in writing', which begins:

- Provide examples of interesting complex sentences. Have fun mimicking the structure with new content as a way of trying it out for size. Try defining the structure as a formula.

Beyond the obvious reaction, 'why should teachers want to provide uninteresting examples of complex sentences?', readers may want to know what defines an 'interesting' complex sentence. What does 'trying it out for size' mean? Having grappled with these questions, teachers and pupils are still no further forward in discovering where the 'learning about language' is to be found in such suggestions.

The tone of the exercises has changed significantly since the textbooks written by Ridout over 50 years ago, but the reason why the work is worth doing in the first place has not itself been stated clearly and made contextually obvious. It is always pleasing to see teachers being advised in government-sponsored documentation to 'have fun'! Greater attention is – rightly – being given to the structuring of text, but this structuring is not then related to the text's purpose. Teachers also want to involve their pupils more securely in the exercises they set for them, and there has been a shift towards applying language work in real contexts, particularly where pupils' writing has been seen. Yet this type of language work is still 'ungrounded'. The 'learning' expected of each exercise is too self-contained. It is not sufficiently revealing about the way language works in general terms, and pupils can draw too few conclusions from it. This unsystematic work could be taking place regularly in considerable numbers of classrooms, yet making relatively little difference to how pupils reflect on the ways they employ language. If such activities are indeed taking place in unrelated 'starter sessions' at the beginning of English lessons – without any sort of progressive overview guiding the choice and staging of such exercises – they are unlikely to contribute to a more assured set of insights into the way language works, fully under the control of pupil writers.

There is no sense of:

- what is the language doing?
- what effect does the language have?
- why is the actual language which has been chosen the most appropriate for the circumstances?

which ought to be the starting points of worthwhile enquiry and interest for both teachers and pupils. Therefore, it will be necessary to select a guiding set of principles upon which all the other suggestions and activities will be fashioned.

Making a case for a particular approach to grammar

This book will be based on a mixture of two approaches to grammar, integrating different notions about language from the past and from more modern times. There is nothing revolutionary or significantly new about the actual choices that have been made. Much of this material has been practised in many schools for 20 to 30 years, but not always in a systematic manner. This approach will be new for some departments, however, and the ways in which the learning takes place will not be familiar.

The major approach to language learning will be through **functional** grammar, based on the work of M. A. K. Halliday, formerly Professor of Linguistics at the University of Sydney. Halliday's research has been extremely important within the development of modern more linguistically based initiatives, such as the National Literacy Strategy in England, although there has been relatively little acknowledgement of its influence in the rationale of that project. The view of grammar promulgated by Halliday is concerned with the dynamics of language as it is used, rather than concentrating on an analytical study of how grammar is acquired.

> A functional approach to grammar is concerned with *how* language works to achieve various *purposes*. It takes account of how the *contexts* in which language is used and the *purposes* of the users give rise to particular texts. It is based on the *functional components of texts* and the *meanings they embody*, rather than on the words and structures which express those meanings. The local details of word form and structure have an important place in the grammar, but they are best understood in terms of the way they fit into larger functional components which can be directly related to the meanings being expressed. (Collerson 1994; emphasis added)

This 'functional' approach will also be combined with the terminology and concepts of **traditional** grammar, but not the 'traditional' ideas based solely on a Latinate model of English. John Collerson, in *Grammar in Teaching* (1997), makes the following case for the adoption of a functional emphasis:

> However, when we consider what kind of grammar best lends itself to teaching in schools, functional grammar can be shown to have some advantages over other modern approaches, as well as over traditional grammar. A functional grammar is concerned with how language works in relation to almost every other aspect of human life. It takes account of the contexts in which language is used, the purposes for using it and the resulting texts. In other words, it starts with the 'big picture', with the meanings embodied in texts, rather than with the details of grammatical structure. It goes some way to overcoming the limitations of other grammars and provides teachers and children with a useful resource for understanding English and for learning to use it more effectively. (Collerson 1997)

Traditional grammar cannot be wholly rejected, however; many of its features will still be extremely helpful in allowing pupils to understand certain linguistic features, not least in the terms it uses for naming parts of the language. But as a describing mechanism for the way language works, it does not have much to offer pupils. Functional grammar has another enormous advantage over traditional approaches; it can be applied to spoken as well as written utterances, in any dialect or level of formality. It also complements and accords with the linguistic stances of both the Bullock Report and the LINC project, so perfunctorily ended by a Conservative government unable to understand that language is a dynamic, living, constantly evolving force in all our lives, requiring the grammar – the manner in which the parts of the language relate to each other – to change accordingly.

Professor Ronald Carter makes the same positive points about the importance of functional grammar in his Introduction to *The LINC Reader*:

> A functional theory of language is a natural complement to influential theories of language development constructed in the 1970s by Professor James Britton and others working to similar principles. These theories make clear the centrality of context, purpose and audience in language use and the salience of this understanding for children's learning. (Carter 1990)

He outlines the main features of functional theory as:

- The making of *meaning* is the reason for the invention, existence and development of language.
- All meanings exist within the context of culture. Cultural values and beliefs determine the purposes, audiences, settings and topics of language.
- Texts, spoken and written, are created and interpreted by making appropriate choices from the language system according to specific purposes, audiences, settings and topics. (*ibid.*)

It may be seen from these principles that language is capable of change. If language serves and is intrinsic to social behaviours and relationships, these are clearly not immutable, fixed factors; they change over time, and different behaviours also take on changed characteristics. It follows that language will also change to reflect these variable social interactions. Variation over time is called *diachronic* variation; variation according to the user – the regional or social circumstances of language – is called *dialectical* variation; variation according to use (the actual functions of the language) is called *diatypic* variation. Merely recognising the potential for change in language in these ways makes nonsense of the idea of one single, universal, overriding grammar.

Thus, the selection of a focused view or approach to grammar, in the manner described above, requires an English department to focus on the implications which stem from that decision. It may be seen that a number of central issues emerge from this commitment to a functional view of language, such as how it works and how it can be learned. In the above quotation from Carter (1990), the words 'context', 'audience' and 'purpose' become paramount, as does the significance of *appropriate choices*. An emphasis on *appropriate choices* reminds teachers that their pupils must be fully active players in the exploration and decision-making of textual interactions in the classroom. This vital consideration confirms an attitude of language teaching which insists that attention should not be focused on the teacher, but stresses:

> its [language's] endless variety of forms and functions and requires a methodology which is not transmissive and teacher-centred but investigative and project-based. (Carter 1990)

It should also remind teachers that reading and writing are inextricably linked. Pupils should practise as much as possible looking into, considering carefully and then discussing the sorts of choices made by the published authors they read, leading to close exploration and control of the meanings they, in their turn, will make in the texts they will construct.

A secondary area of interest, leading on from the first, yet demanding considerable attention in its own right, is the notion and central importance of *text* itself. Halliday has the following to offer to our understanding of this fundamental idea:

> Social interaction typically takes a linguistic form, which we call *text*. A text is the product of infinitely many simultaneous and successive choices in meaning, and is realised as lexicogrammatical structure or 'wording'. The environment of the text is the context of situation, which is an instance of the social context, or *situation type*. The situation type is a semiotic construct which is structured in terms of *field*, *tenor* and *mode*; the text-generating activity, the role relationships of the participants, and the rhetorical modes they are adopting. (Halliday 1978; emphasis in original)

While some of the technical jargon contained in the above extract may, at first sight, be thought to be daunting, it should not take teachers of English too long to rework this difficult text into straightforward meanings. The words *field, tenor* and *mode* can be illustrated immediately by close consideration of the following passage:

> *Carry On* humour was born in 1957 when the low-budget Norman Huddis comedy was shot for £74,000 and was the third most popular film of 1958. The film was *Carry On Sergeant*, the first ever film in the highly successful Carry On comedy series – now an acclaimed British institution.
>
> Forget sharp satire. The Carry On series began and continued with vulgar, but never crude, humour and jokes which could be seen a mile off. This predictability was and still is all part of the fun.
>
> The early films were always suggestive and never explicit. Peter Rogers, producer of every film in the series, himself commented: 'We talk a lot about sex in our films. But nothing ever happens'.
>
> Carry On actors soon became clichés of their own caricatures: Jim Dale, the nice young man; Charles Hawtrey, always sexually ambiguous; Hattie Jacques, matronly and in control; Kenneth Williams, the snobbish intellectual; Peter Butterworth, the frustrated old man and Sid James with that unforgettable yak yak laugh. (Davies 2001)

An analysis of this passage, in terms of functional grammar, might be carried out in the following manner:

- **Field** (what the text is about – 'the text generating activity' according to Halliday): The passage is concerned with offering some insight into and explanation of a collection of films with similar content in a comic genre. The reader might expect some words about the background and history of these films – 'was born', 'was the third', 'began', 'were always', 'first ever'. There will be language of cause and effect – 'was born ... when', 'began and continued with ... but', 'this predictability was and still is ...', 'We talk a lot about. .. But ...'. There are likely to be technical, sometimes even jargonistic, terms: 'low-budget', 'comedy series' 'producer'. The passage deals with a series of films and people, and will therefore contain a high density of names (nouns and noun phrases); for example, '*Carry On*', 'comedy', 'Norman Huddis', 'comedy series', all the actors' names. Part of the explanation is to inform the audience of the different characteristics of those featured, which means a high proportion of adjectives: 'popular', 'first', 'acclaimed', 'sharp', 'vulgar', 'crude', 'matronly', 'young', 'snobbish', 'frustrated', 'old', etc.
- **Tenor** (the different roles taken up by the writer and the reader – and the relationship that might exist between them – what Halliday calls 'role

relationship of the participants'): The writer obviously has some expertise and knowledge about film, writing from a position of authority, but is not necessarily an academic in that area (there are a number of informal colloquialisms – 'Forget sharp satire', 'be seen a mile off'). The reader is probably not an expert, but knows something about this series of films. The reader wants to be entertained as well as informed by choosing this sort of text (there are much tougher and more linguistically challenging film books available). There is an assumption that the reader is aware of the roles the various actors play, as these are not explained further.

- **Mode** (the way/manner in which the text is made – the Hallidayan 'rhetorical mode'): This text is clearly written, and certainly not spoken. It is tightly organised into short paragraphs. The stages are predictable and typical of such text. The colloquialisms suggest a more human and less academic approach.

Pupils too can begin to comprehend and explore these same issues and ideas, not, of course, in quite these words, but presented to them in staged and appropriate ways. Indeed, pupils' understanding of this material is essential in a balanced learning programme of language and language in use.

The study of functional grammar, as seen above, also supports pupils in making better relationships in their own minds with the clearer understanding of the idea of audiences. They should be assisted in becoming more aware of the demands and responsibilities placed on them as writers to meet the needs of their audiences. The importance of paying close attention to the **tenor** of what they write should be very much part of the way in which they ask questions of their own written pieces. 'What does my audience expect of this sort of writing?' and 'How closely have I adhered to what I know of this genre?' are the starting points for ensuring that the expected characteristics are in place. This critical awareness should not be constraining, however. Writers have to be sure that they have offered their audiences what those audiences have come to expect, but sometimes only up to a certain point. Adventurous and creative writers use the genre outlines available to them, and then deviate from and subvert normal expectations. The realistic first priority for many teachers working with the majority of pupils, however, is to make sure that the fundamental principles of the required genres are known and understood by those pupils.

Another implication deriving directly from the selection of functional grammar is its emphasis on *choice.* When language users recognise that different social discourses are shaped by the language structures (syntax) and morphology (words) of the text, they will begin to realise that subtle changes in meaning are possible through the smallest of adjustments. With this understanding, readers should be prepared to look very closely at what writers have written, recognising that the printed text in front of them was constructed with enormous care in the first place before undergoing a number of editorial 'choosing' processes. Similarly, as well as having something to say in their own writing, they should also be made aware of the structuring possibilities and alternatives available to them, from which they can draw in order to make the most deliberate meanings they can.

The selection of functional grammar as the focus of language work also makes it possible for teachers to give their pupils the supportive assistance of *genre knowledge.* In the past, genre referred almost exclusively to different forms of literary writing, but the term has widened gradually so that it now applies to almost any sort of written text. The word 'genre' derives from the same root word as 'gender', meaning class or group containing similar attributes. Texts which have been brought into the world to fulfil similar *purposes* seem to share a large number of similar linguistic features. By attending to, and helping pupils pay closer attention to, the *purposes* of texts it should be possible to enable them to recognise the 'family' of linguistic qualities to which different texts belong.

The research of M. A. K. Halliday and his team at the University of Sydney suggested, among others, the following propositions about the nature of genre:

- that forms of text (genres) are the results of processes of social production;
- that, given the relative stability of social structures, forms of text produced in and by specific social institutions, that is the resultant genres, will attain a certain degree of stability and persistence over time;
- that consequently, texts in their generic form are not unique creations uttered each time by an individual (or individuals) expressing an inner meaning, but are rather the effects of the action of individual social agents acting both within the bounds of their social history and the constraints of particular contexts, and with a knowledge of existing generic types;
- that genres have specifiable linguistic characteristics which are neither fully determined nor largely under the control of individual speakers or writers. (Kress 1989)

Accepting the functional approach to grammar suggested by this book may present problems to some teachers of English. The National Literacy Strategy in primary schools first promoted on a large scale the learning and understanding of different non-fiction text types through the principles of 'genre theory', based on the work of Derewianka (1990) and developed through the Excel project of Wray and Lewis (1997). Most teachers have been comfortable about teaching a genre-based approach to non-fiction, but they have not considered it appropriate or helpful to extend the same approach to works of fiction. The final proposition in the above list will clearly be a challenge to many who believe that part of their professional responsibility is to encourage young people to explore and discover new textual possibilities through their English lessons.

> From the point of view of both 'English' and of post-structuralism, genre theory is seen as advocating a view of texts and of the production of texts which is overly deterministic, reductive and mechanistic. Genre theory shares with liberal individualism a view of individuals as 'centred'; however, the former sees individuals as socially 'produced', in structures of power, and in ideology, and therefore as socially 'centred', whereas the latter sees individuals as biologically and psychologically produced, and as psychologically centred. (*ibid.*)

Integrating the study of genre into English studies

Figure 2.1 should offer some help in seeing how these features can be integrated into classroom work, but the following ideas may also be discussed with pupils to help them begin to gain some background in thinking about text in this recommended manner.

There are degrees of difficulty in considering issues of genre. For instance, not all texts are representative of 'pure' genres; genres regularly overlap in a very large number of texts. Pupils should not be led to believe that they can regard individual texts as neat little packages of separate genres; that is not how language is employed in real-life situations. We rarely pursue single-issue purposes in our discourses.

Some genres, however, are more straightforward and directly obvious than others. One such, now familiar to primary pupils from the earliest days of their schooling, due to the National Literacy Strategy, is the 'instruction' or 'procedural' (as in 'how to proceed') genre. This sort of text is employed frequently in a whole range of social contexts. It is the material of cooking recipes and other 'how to make things' circumstances; the rules of games, the way of informing people how to find their destination, and many road signs. A close consideration of the 'purposes' of instruction will enable pupils to see how certain parts of language are prominently foregrounded, and make good sense of the regularly patterned structuring:

Literacy	Language	English
The fullest insight into the 'languages' culture in which we live –

The total repertoire of controlled, appropriate and purposeful EXPRESSION (speaking and writing) or MEANING MAKING (listening and reading) across the whole range of social and learning discourses embodied in TEXTS

So – in practice – if purpose is to **instruct**, that usually means that the text will be constructed:

if purpose is to **describe**, that usually means that the text will contain:

– if the purpose is to **narrate**, that usually means the text will be written: | the 'material'/ components of ALL texts

words/phrases/ clauses/sentences signs/symbols images gestures

ways of conveying meaning through agreed culturally based linguistic structures in purposeful discourses called TEXTS

● in imperative voice (second person)
● in present tense
● in sequential development
● in short, pointed sentences

● many adjectives/adverbs
● adjectival/adverbial phrases
● metaphors and similes
● viewpoint in first/third person/past or present tense

● in first–third person
● in the past tense
● with variable sentence length (genre dependent)
● possibly including dialogue | The name of the language.

A school subject, defined through National Curriculum Orders/historical practice
– **in Key Stage 1**
usually (pre NLS) meaning initial instruction in reading and writing of all mostly fiction texts (some speaking and listening) – recently broader range of texts
– **in Key Stage 2**
usually (before NLS) increasingly concerned with literary texts (narrative fiction/poetry/a little drama – personal recount/descriptive writing) – and some non-fiction study as part of growing literacy knowledge
– **in Key Stages 3 and 4**
usually about increasing attention on literary texts – poetic/metaphoric/dramatic – classical literary canon – some study of modern fiction/media texts – increasingly critical/evaluative writing/ some personal – imaginative, argument/reasoning writing (imagine/explore/entertain inform/explain/describe persuade/argue/advise analyse/review/comment) |

So – within our literacy culture – huge numbers of **text types** are intended to fulfil particular purposes, by employing linguistic devices in particular ways:

● they might be – describing/persuading/reflecting/commenting/explaining/recounting/ evaluating/exploring/abusing/inciting.
● some are *narrating* stories or events – to excite (action adventure)/move (love)/ impress (describe)/frighten (horror)/amuse (comedy)/tease (suspense)/forecast (science fiction)/reflect (war)

Learning is intrinsically bound up and contained/framed in the discourses in which it takes place.
An example – in chemistry – could see the pupil possibly expected to:

● *inform* the teacher of specific facts
● *recount* the details of an experiment
● *explain* what has taken place in a chemical reaction
● *describe* what was seen as a result of the reaction
● *evaluate* how successful an experiment might have been

all different linguistic tasks – involving separate/ distinguishable grammars – fulfilling different purposes

Figure 2.1 Language use

- An instruction is intended to bring about a result, an outcome – therefore, it will place great emphasis on the <u>processes</u> (the verbs, as we will probably more easily recognise them). The verbs will be prominent and about different activities.
- An instruction is about achieving an outcome in the most direct possible way; it will therefore be constructed in unadorned prose, without unnecessary detail.
- An instruction takes place in a continual present tense – even if whatever is to come about will be realised in the future, because it has a 'nowness' about it. The tense of the discourse is clearly established.
- An instruction is a direct communication from the instructor to the instructed; consequently, it will be conducted in the second person of the verb (the 'you' voice), and sometimes (depending on the urgency or tone) in the imperative, where the discourse will become more than an instruction and move up a notch to become a command.
- An instruction text will often be dependent upon a sequence of procedures. Many written instances of such texts will be deliberately set out in chronological/developmental stages, demarcated by numbered paragraphs, or some similar manner of suggesting instalments;
- An instruction text will sometimes be used to bring about a recognised, specific end-product, which might well appear as an illustration to assist the maker in achieving an outcome very close to the original.

Having been encouraged to explore the likely content of an instruction text – in the context of considering its *purposes* – and having compiled, through their discussions, a 'checklist' similar to the one above, pupils need to see examples of such texts, to discover whether their ideas are borne out by real experience. Two short examples of the above might be:

- The four letters written in white in the middle of the road at a road junction: 'STOP'.
- First heat the oil in a large saucepan, add the onion and let it cook gently for about 10 minutes without colouring. Then add the garlic and cook for another minute. Now add the tomato purée and rosemary, stir for a minute and then pour in the beans, together with 3 pints (1.75 litres) of the reserved water (topping up the liquid, if necessary) and some salt. Now bring everything up to simmering point and simmer very gently, partially covered, for about an hour until the beans are tender. (Smith 2001)

Analysis of these texts relative to the criteria set out for instructional/ procedural text types above produces the following findings:

'STOP'

- Is the focus on the processes (verbs) and are they action verbs? – Most definitely: the only word is a verb, and an 'action' (although, strictly speaking, it is meant to bring about inaction, following previous action!).
- Is it unadorned/direct? – Without doubt: it is one word long.
- Is the text in the present tense? – Yes: 'stop' (not stopping/stopped etc.).
- Is it in the second person? – Yes: in the imperative voice (no use of the 'you' pronoun, it is 'assumed').
- Is this passage sequenced, built in stages? – Not applicable in this case.
- Is there an illustration/picture? – Not applicable in this case.

The Delia Smith recipe

- Is the focus on the processes, and are the verbs active? – Yes: the passage is dependent on them, and the majority are activities – 'heat', 'let . . . cook', 'colouring', 'add', 'cook', 'stir', 'pour', 'topping', 'bring', 'simmer', etc.
- Is the text unadorned/direct? – Yes: all 'extra' details are necessary to bring about the processes as efficiently as possible.
- Is the text in the present tense? – Yes: 'First heat . . . add the onion', etc.
- Is this passage sequenced, built in stages? – Yes, 'first . . .', 'then . . .', 'now . . .', etc.
- Is there an illustration/picture? – Yes: the finished product (a bowl of 'Tuscan bean and pasta soup with rosemary') is illustrated on the facing page in the original text.

These findings suggest quite strongly that both of these texts qualify as good examples of the instructional, or procedural.

An interesting activity that pupils might also be asked to undertake would be to consider what the alternative possibilities of both of these texts might be. Instead of 'STOP', imagine the following road sign:

You are about to arrive at a road junction. There is a strong likelihood that you might hit a vehicle passing on the main road if you do not take some precautions, such as slowing down, or even stopping.

It is easy to see that the purposefulness of the 'STOP' sign has some distinct advantages.

And the recipe:

I would like to suggest that the oil will cause beneficial changes to the other ingredients if it is hotter than it will be if poured directly from the bottle. It can be made hot by applying heat of some kind, either on an electrical hob or one powered by gas. Once at a critical temperature, the other ingredients should be added in the following order, etc.

It is important that pupils are asked from the outset to suggest what the 'purposes' of a text (such as the procedural one described above), might be. From this abstract analysis, without examples of text available, pupils in Key Stage 3 should be able to construct a set of criteria, similar to the above, to apply as a checklist to real texts deemed to belong to that 'genre'. A selection of such texts should then be put to the test to see how closely the criteria have been satisfied. This set of exercises will be entirely practical, guided by a teacher prompting where necessary, but actually led and carried out by the pupils discovering for themselves the features of genre. Through this process pupils should be able to construct a worthwhile and helpful 'writing frame' for supporting any writing they may wish to compose for themselves in that genre. (It is worth noting that these are not the same as the closed, rather mechanical writing frames found in a number of published resources which largely control the pupils' writing by beginning sentences for them, or sequencing events in a strict manner.)

In order to emphasise the point I made earlier about whole texts rarely being of one genre, readers should note that the following paragraph, written on the same page above the Delia Smith recipe, would not fit the criteria of instruction/procedural genre:

This is Tuscany in a bowl, with all those lovely Italian flavours in a big, hefty soup – perfect for the winter months with a light main course to follow. Alternatively, it is a complete lunch with just some cheese and a salad to follow.

This passage is structured largely around verbs derived from 'to be' (existing verbs – 'is'), and contains a number of words adding attractive, extra detail to persuade the reader to pay greater attention – 'lovely Italian', 'big, hefty', 'perfect', 'light', 'complete', etc.). This sort of writing is more akin to the 'persuasive' genre. It precedes the recipe to entice readers to stop at that point and take further notice of what is on the page. The construction of two different text types on the same page is not unusual, especially where there is likely to be an overlap of similar but slightly different purposes. School textbooks often have more than one genre on each page, and pupils should become accustomed to discovering a far greater sense of what is happening in their books if they have some idea of the different *purposes* of different parts of the page.

Applying similar genre knowledge to the writing of different types of narrative

While teachers of English are likely to be interested in the grammatical features of non-fiction texts, and want to explore their pupils' knowledge of this area of language structure, much of their real concern will be about the nature of fiction materials. The Key Stage 3 *Framework for Teaching English: Years 7, 8 and 9* requires a great deal of attention to non-fiction texts (e.g. Year 7 SL 13); yet there are far fewer suggestions relating to the sorts of text seen more often in English lessons. Departments already familiar with the implications of functional grammar, and preparing lessons and devising learning based on that approach, would be in a stronger position to enable their pupils to move easily into studying different fictional forms.

Readers should refer once again to Figure 2.1. Most works of prose fiction are written in a genre known as *narrative*. Beverley Derewianka in *Exploring How Texts Work* (1990) explains some of the readily identifiable linguistic features of narrative texts:

One of the major functions of language is to enable us to represent the world – and not only the real world but imaginary, possible worlds. The world is made up of people, places, objects, animals, plants, concepts, machines and so on. But the world is not static – it also involves events and happenings. We could describe the world in terms of **processes** and **participants** in those processes. We could see a text as representing those participants and processes in language, e.g.

The children	were reading	their novels.
participant	process	participant

The processes represent 'what's going on in the world'. In traditional grammar, processes are referred to as 'verbs'. We may generally think of verbs as 'doing' words. But this is rather vague and not entirely accurate. There are many types of processes going on in the world:

- the 'doings': the actions and happenings we observe taking place around us (he walked, they drove, it rained), referred to as the *material processes*;
- the processes that humans engage in with their intellect and senses, referred to as *mental processes*, e.g.
  believing, knowing (*processes of cognition*)
  seeing, observing (*processes of perception*)
  fearing, enjoying (*processes of feeling/affect*)

- the 'talking' or verbal processes (he said, she accused, they promised).

Each of these processes refers to a different type of reality:

- the reality of the 'real world' (*material*)
- the reality as perceived and interpreted through the senses (*mental*)
- the reality we construct through language (*verbal*). (Derewianka 1990)

This lengthy quotation is necessary in order to gain a good overview of which similar *functions* most writers of narratives are performing through the selection of the language to bring about a broad range of texts we recognise as narratives.

But narrative writers also have other intentions, besides those already described, realised through appropriate linguistic structures:

- the writer of a *horror* narrative will want to frighten the reading audience, and draw on a vocabulary and structuring devices capable of fulfilling that purpose;
- the author of a *mystery* or *suspense* narrative will want to mystify or tease the reader, perhaps using the language of evasion;
- those writers attempting to construct *action adventure* narrative texts will wish to leave the reader with a feeling of excitement and energy achieved through very deliberate linguistic effects.

Authors may want to include, for particular purposes of their narrative intention, passages of detailed description, or, conversely, write in a tight, spare, focused manner. These are the sorts of linguistic issues in texts that we want our pupils to notice, and pay considerable attention to, as they attempt to discover and ascertain the fullest possible range of meanings in a process known as *reading*. They are also meant to be the materials our pupils should be selecting and moulding to construct their own texts in writing. These matters are explored and exemplified in Chapter 6, about using grammar knowledge to improve writing.

Ultimately, however, the study of language in the classroom will have genuine effect only in a context where pupils are able to read the texts of others because *they are interested in them, want to discover their meanings* and are ready to write because *they have something worthwhile to convey.*

CHAPTER 3

Creating a School Context for Language Teaching

The new grammar teaching presents a number of pedagogic challenges for both teachers and pupils. Foremost among these is a challenge to present grammar in the classroom in ways which avoid the worst excesses of formalism without losing sight of the fact that grammar is systematically organised. (Carter 1990)

If the majority of English teachers regard the primary function of the subject as the personal and social development of pupils, then for language study to be embraced it would have to be clear how such content fitted into teachers' beliefs and values. (Poulson 1998)

Wanting pupils to acquire a sophisticated knowledge of language, and to read and write for pleasure, are not and should never be regarded as incompatible. Recently however, and particularly since the Key Stage 3 English and literacy strands were introduced into secondary schools to continue the work of the National Literacy Strategy from primary schools, there has been much published discontent and continuous, often discontented discussion. Much of the most critical material claims that learning about language use in school and activities such as writing creatively can never be complementary.

Some of the discussion has been intemperately unhelpful:

It's depressing to see so many English teachers welcoming the National Literacy Strategy (NLS) into their departments in secondary schools. When John Rae wrote some years ago that 'The overthrow of grammar coincided with the acceptance of the equivalence of creative writing in social behaviour', the former head teacher of Westminster School was merely reflecting an agenda that brought about the NLS. When Melanie Phillips wrote that 'The Revolt against teaching the rules of grammar became part of the wider repudiation of external forms of authority' in her slight, mean and underpowered little book of 1996 she was merely repeating that agenda.

Out of this – it isn't thinking but more a kind of pensioned off sublime, all sentimental, kitsch and nasty – there came the NLS to our primary schools and, despite its failures there, it is now being extended into the secondary sector. The fact that the initiative is merely a half-baked set of reactionary prejudices overcooked by expensive PR should have been enough to for it to have been thrown into the slop bin by now. (Marshall 2002)

Other comment has been more measured and thoughtful:

We are entitled to ask why language is such a matter of political anxiety from authorities. Why aren't they so anxious about art or biology? Politicians are not to be heard lamenting the fact that people's sense of the visual is poor or that most people don't know what their pulmonary artery is. Language seems to be the target of political and social anxieties. Most of the policies brought in are a response to those anxieties and not to the fascinating questions of e.g. what writing is for, how we enjoy it, why we enjoy it, how language sticks together in our conversations and writing, how every utterance takes place within a social situation with real participants, how the language itself will always be shot through with the needs and desires of these participants. (Rosen 2002)

Or:

I am thinking here not of language and literature, but of what we may call, for the sake of argument, functional English and creative English. Each is a sub-set of the vastly complex phenomenon that is the English language. Each has a legitimate and necessary place on the curriculum, and should be taught from the early years of schooling onwards. They should, however, be taught and assessed in quite different ways. (MacDonald 2000)

However, whatever the quality of the criticism, some of it is based on a fundamental misunderstanding of the reasons why grammar has been re-emphasised in the English curriculum, or what the Key Stage 3 English NLS strand is designed to bring about. These misunderstandings are certainly fuelled by the clumsy manner in which the KS 3 English *Framework* (DfEE 2001a) is written, partly by the mythologies of centralised 'control of the English curriculum' that have persisted since the introduction of the primary strategy, and from the contents of many of the training materials published by the NLS. The materials produced on the teaching of grammar in the secondary English programme have been made very vulnerable by not being aligned intellectually or pedagogically to any particular view of grammar.

Establishing a school-based rationale

Schools have to establish for themselves a coherent and workable set of reasons why they are adopting a curriculum with a large grammatically based linguistic content. They need to publish, or certainly agree, on a set of assumptions that will underpin their approach and make clear to themselves, their pupils – and, possibly, colleagues in other subject areas – what learning and attainment they want their pupils to acquire.

> Within each school and in curriculum documents there should be clear guidelines about the use of grammatical terms, though they should not be too rigid or dogmatic. However, the most important thing is not the terminology but the development of children's understanding of how the language works and how to use it effectively in context. To try to achieve this just through the traditional grammar would be a circumscribed approach; it's better to draw upon the wider perspective of the modern grammars as well. One can go so far with traditional grammar but it is limited; the functional approach embodies a richer view of language, to which children should be given access. (Collerson 1997)

Yet many current teachers of English in secondary schools are unaware of the 'modern grammars', how they resemble or differ from the 'traditional grammars', and what the most effective selections from 'traditional' or 'modern' approaches might be.

In her eminently practical book *A Grammar Companion for Primary Teachers* (1998), Beverley Derewianka suggests the following utterly straightforward rationale and assumptions that help to contextualise why the study of grammar could, once again, be appropriate and necessary in schools:

Why learn about grammar?
- to be able to reflect on how the English language works;
- to have shared language for talking about the main features of the English language;
- to understand how grammatical structures create different kinds of meaning;
- to examine patterns of language and word choices to critically analyse texts;
- to be able to use language effectively, appropriately and accurately.

Assumptions

- Language is a dynamic, complex system of resources for making meaning. Students should be encouraged to explore it as a fascinating phenomenon which is central to their lives.
- Language reflects the culture in which it is used. It is not a neutral medium, but expresses certain world-views, values, beliefs and attitudes.
- Language changes from situation to situation, depending on the social purposes for which it is being used, the subject matter, who is involved, and whether the language is spoken or written.
- The emphasis in language study is on how people use authentic language in various contexts in real life to achieve their purposes. The particular focus will be on the language needed for successful participation in school contexts.
- A knowledge of grammar can help us to critically evaluate our own texts and those of others (e.g. identifying point of view; examining how language can be manipulated to achieve certain effects and position the reader in a particular way; knowing how language can be used to construct a particular identity or way of viewing the world).
- The approach to grammar should not have the effect of excluding or marginalising students who speak a social dialect which is different from Standard English. Different varieties of English are to be respected and maintained, while extending the students' ability to use appropriate registers in specific situations (e.g. written texts in school and workplace contexts). (Derewianka 1998)

Had the new Key Stage 3 English materials offered such a solid contextual 'framing' as the Derewianka model, English departments would have been in a more secure position to implement a clearer view of grammar/language studies. By comparison, the NLS documentation is very clumsy. The KS 3 English *Framework* has been compiled to outline an entitlement curriculum for all pupils in Years 7 to 9. This facility was deemed necessary because of the wild variation in content of English schemes of work from school to school. The programme was also designed to ensure that the improved expectations of children's levels of attainment during the primary phase were continued into the secondary sector. Too often, however, in its attempts to ensure a reasonable coverage, the Strategy has been written in an inexplicable shorthand that has caused understandable confusion and sometimes anger in the teachers whom it is meant to be supporting.

An example is to be found on page 22 of the *Framework*:

Sentence level
Sentence construction and punctuation
Pupils should be taught to:

1. extend their use and control of complex sentences by:
   a. recognising and using subordinate clauses;
   b. exploring the functions of subordinate clauses, e.g. relative clauses such as 'which I bought' or adverbial clauses such as 'having finished his lunch';
   c. deploying subordinate clauses in a variety of positions within the sentence;
2. expand nouns and noun phrases, e.g. by using a prepositional phrase, etc.

It is easy to see how this sort of 'instruction' (which is what a number of English teachers think they are being told to do!) has the potential to lend itself to the narrowest interpretation, likely – in turn – to draw the worst possible criticism. It *is* undoubtedly important that pupils have a sense of and insight into the use of complex sentences, containing – as they do – subordinate clauses. There is every possibility, however, that this requirement is then dutifully dealt with in classrooms by becoming the central focus in one or two starter sessions, more than likely in a decontextualised manner, resulting in the least impact on subsequent writing improvement of the pupils. This particular objective is then 'ticked off' the checklist and is regarded as having been sufficiently well covered.

While the words 'exploring the functions' and 'extending control' suggest more reasonable contexts for wanting to study such material, certainly better than the reasons for similar study in the 1950s, the actual exercises employed have changed very little. Of course, not all English teachers or departments will take this minimalist route to incorporating the material of language learning into their teaching, but unless it is successfully discussed or modelled in its more potentially influential and relevant manifestation, teachers who have not seen its true capabilities will not stumble on them readily. The training materials sent out to LEAs, designed to assist teachers in making clearer sense of the grammatical objectives, were very inadequate in this respect, and merely confirmed the worst sceptical viewpoints that they were witnessing a return to something like 'prescriptive grammar'.

The second point to consider is the notion that the KS 3 *Framework* is a set of non-negotiable, controlling instructions to be imposed at all costs in a prescribed manner. This interpretation has to be debunked. The KS 3 *Framework* recommends in an explicit manner how the objectives should be most effectively employed:

> The notion that literacy embedded in the objectives is much more than simply the acquisition of 'basic skills' which is sometimes implied by the word; it encompasses the ability to recognise, understand and manipulate the conventions of language, and to develop pupils' ability to use language imaginatively and flexibly. (DfEE 2002a, p. 9)

And:

> The list of objectives does not imply that teachers should approach them in isolation or teach them in a reductive way. . . Teachers are encouraged to find ways of clustering together complementary objectives. (*ibid.*, p. 11)

Yet there is no suggestion anywhere in the documentation that the objectives are separate, stand-alone requirements, to be learned in a slavish manner and tested regularly. They are recommended areas of study, to be integrated into programmes of study – or highlighted when identified as obvious needs to assist particular pupils – assessed through the degree of confidence in which pupils employ them. Graham Frater, ex-HMI Staff Inspector for English, who has recently undertaken research into the relative literacy success of boys, goes further, and has stated quite clearly that departments which do not organise their planning in the most focused manner, basing it solely on their pupils' needs, are unlikely to see real improvement. While the following statement is made in the context of primary planning, nevertheless it may be applied just as surely to the planning of the secondary English department:

> Least progress (in literacy) had been made where staffs were most anxious about, or preoccupied by covering the recommended content of the Framework's termly programme. Most progress was made where staff were confident about their own teaching and where planning – without ignoring specific content – was concerned more with skills, principles and their application to real examples of language use. (Frater 2000)

The *Framework* document does not deal specifically with why the strategy was devised; such intentions seem to be assumed. Therefore, I deemed it helpful to set out what I believed to be the main purposes of the Key Stage 3 Literacy Strategy when I was writing about it at the time of its introduction. In my view it was designed to:

- provide a clearer entitlement curriculum for pupils in English across Key Stage 3;
- help track more firmly progression in English across the Key Stage;
- make the study of language as the conveyor of meaning more important;
- give greater attention to learning through language and literacy engagements;
- pay increased attention to word level, sentence level and text level considerations, and use them as more secure foundations of language learning;
- continue the sorts of learning to which pupils have become accustomed in Key Stages 1 and 2 in to the secondary school;
- 'make the transparent more apparent', i.e. to make clearer and more obvious to teachers and pupils the sorts of practices and events currently familiar in English classrooms, but not always framed and foregrounded as learning activities. (Dean 2002)

If other teachers of English regarded the English strand of the strategy in this manner, they would want to insist that increased attention is expected to be paid to:

- language and the ways it works, the functions it performs and its contribution to the broadest making of meaning in reading and writing;
- learning – planned and anticipated by teachers – shared with and understood by pupils (but never intended to exclude the spontaneous learning events that will always continue to emerge in all good English lessons).

The adoption of these priorities would point to a necessary emphasis being applied to the very conscious scrutiny of the linguistic features in texts, by pupils of all abilities, to bring about more careful listening or reading (to focus on the precise meanings of what has been uttered) – and more deliberate speaking or writing (to ensure that utterances being made are wholly intended).

Creating a secure departmental rationale for the teaching of grammar

In *Teaching English in the Key Stage 3 Literacy Strategy* (Dean 2002), I suggested that English departments are likely to make more progress in language learning with all their pupils if they have already discussed together and collaboratively agreed the sorts of reasonable, broadly defined outcomes their work should be attempting to bring about. English has always been a subject bedevilled by difficulties when it comes to those who teach it focusing on exactly what it is for. It is worth reviewing what Robert Protherough and Judith Atkinson had to say in their chapter 'Shaping the image of an English teacher' in Susan Brindley's seminal text *Teaching English* (Brindley 1994). They state:

> To teach a subject that in many ways is more than a subject and that has major repercussions outside the classroom walls, has imposed a special responsibility on English teachers... Because there is no generally agreed body of subject knowledge, the boundaries of the subject are notoriously unclear and cannot be neatly defined.

This was certainly how English teachers viewed their role and how they described the nature of their work a few years ago, but disinterested readers would have great difficulty explaining the exact nature of that work from the evidence of the above passage. At the time there was a genuine belief that:

> English has a special power to challenge conventions, institutions, governments, business interests – any established system. This resides in the fact that English is concerned with uncontrollable power of a shared language that we all speak and the uncontrollable responses to what we read. The work of English teaching involves continual pressing for the expression of alternative ideas, inviting challenge to received opinions, seeking strong personal responses, establishing debate. The teacher's special relationship with students depends on democratic openness, not on knowing the answers. The subject matter of English lessons is likely to draw on the actual interests and experiences of pupils, where they may be more informed than those who teach them. (*ibid.*)

Yet nowhere in that chapter was there any direct statement, or any sort of easy inference to be made, that English teaching had the central functions of improving reading, writing and speaking and listening. Those intentions were vaguely implied, but never highlighted in any specific manner.

I want to assert that English teachers have to move on beyond that modest ambition of merely wanting to improve, what George Keith calls 'the four gerunds' of English: reading, writing, speaking and listening. I believe that teachers should outline and describe to themselves what 'sorts' of readers, or writers, or speakers or listeners they should be attempting to encourage. The head of an English department should ask, 'after five years of pupils undertaking compulsory work in this department what sorts of readers, writers, speakers and listeners would we be expecting to fashion as a result?' 'What linguistically based characteristics or "qualities" would this department ideally expect to see in the majority of its pupils, of whatever ability, that could indicate to ourselves, and all other interested parties, that our work had been successful?' (I am not necessarily considering the numerical outcomes of test or examination results in these questions, although a tighter focus on any shared characteristics which the department was collaboratively intending to encourage would go some way towards contributing to more positive outcomes likely to relieve that continual pressure.) The sorts of features, characteristics or 'qualities' I am alluding to do not appear in the Key Stage 3 Strategy, nor the National Curriculum documentation (although the Strategy goes some way towards suggesting final outcomes of its adoption by offering outlines of what it describes as 'shrewd and fluent independent readers', 'confident writers' and 'effective speakers and writers' (DfEE 2001a). They are extra features that the department has to formulate for itself, but they could be developed and furthered in any department very easily through the focused planning of groups of carefully selected objectives. Indeed, they would offer a much more coherent rationale for planning, giving real shape to the selection and combination of the objectives, not illustrated anywhere in the supportive materials yet published for the Strategy.

The following suggested 'qualities' of writers and readers are offered here as devices for initiating discussion about setting up the sorts of focus discussed above. Thus a department might claim that the following 'qualities' – all those aspects of linguistic engagement that pupils have learned to activate, whatever the circumstances – are those they seek to bring about when they are teaching their pupils to write.

This school or subject department promotes a view of writing that believes:

1. A writer knows that writing is a purposeful, controlled, deliberate, text-making construct – different from, but related to, speaking.
2. A writer knows that all writing should be designed to meet the needs of real or imagined audiences.
3. A writer knows that writing should be framed within recognisable text types or genres, and their possible combinations.
4. A writer knows that more precise and effective writing can be achieved through informed grammatical and linguistic choices.
5. A writer knows that writing can be compiled more carefully when modelled through attentive critical reading.
6. A writer knows that writing is a process, capable of continued improvement.
7. A writer knows that writing can be used to articulate, rehearse, explore

and consolidate ideas, concepts, theories, speculation and knowledge.

8. A writer knows that more successful writing can be prepared through preliminary talk.
9. A writer knows that writing skills can be improved through self-evaluation of and reflection on progress.

Shaping a departmental view of writing in these terms explains why the teaching of grammar has such a significant part to play. Statement 4 (A writer knows that more precise and effective writing can be achieved through informed grammatical and linguistic choices) is specifically about pupils securing sufficient grammatical knowledge to enable them to make the sorts of 'informed' choices expected. (The relationship with functional grammar and its insistence on pupil 'choices' is also made quite clear.) Statements 1, 3, 5 and 6 also include high expectations of pupils calling on a good grasp of grammatical skills to impact strongly on their writing development:

- *Statement 1* is about 'control'; the pupil needs to be very aware of each decision to do with the way the text is constructed.
- *Statement 3* has to do with 'genre'; the pupil needs to be aware that genres are conventions of certain grammatical patterns and syntactical arrangements to serve particular purposes.
- *Statement 5* expects the writer to have paid careful attention to the structuring and features of the textual models on which his or her own new text will be built, to build a framing support from them.
- *Statement 6* is more to do with processes, but still has within it the expectation that, as writers build their texts, they should put increasingly tougher questions to them, possibly including those enquiries to do with grammatical organisation.

Formating writing tasks in this manner means that pupils will need to be immersed in grammatical issues to acquire the levels of 'control' – and, through them, a level of much greater success – offered by this approach.

This book is also concerned with how grammar knowledge can contribute to improving reading capability, and it is therefore important to have the same sort of overriding framework to focus what the department is seeking to bring about in its pupils in that particular area of linguistic learning. The following offers a set of learning outcomes to do with reading, in the same manner as those for writing.

This school or subject department believes that:

1. A reader knows that reading is a complex, intellectual endeavour,

requiring the reader to draw on a range of active meaning-making skills.

2. A reader searches previous knowledge of other texts to enable the effective meaning-making of the text being read.
3. A reader is aware that texts are constructed for particular purposes, for identifiable audiences and within recognisable text types or genres.
4. A reader can usually predict the ways texts are likely to work and develop, and can use reading to confirm or adjust those predictions, depending on how typically the text unfolds.
5. A reader is critically active before becoming involved in the substantial body of any text.
6. A reader is able to activate a growing repertoire of critical and analytical questions in engagements with new and unfamiliar texts.
7. A reader knows increasingly how to interact appropriately with a variety of text types/genres for particular purposes.
8. A reader is aware that an important way of demonstrating reading progression is through raising more complex questions about the same text.
9. A reader is aware that learning to read is a lifelong process.
10. A reader is aware that other readers do not always read and make meanings in the same ways.
11. A reader can explain why a text might not satisfy the task to which it has been put, or been rejected unfinished.
12. A reader knows that reading improves through monitoring and reflection on one's own ability and progress.

A good understanding – and the conscious taking 'notice' – of grammar will be beneficial for pupils learning with regard to Statements 1, 3, 4, 6 and 7 in particular:

- *Statement 1*, which emphasises the range of 'active meaning-making skills' undertaken by readers, would include the explicit seeking of grammatical patterns.
- *Statement 3* recognises that genres are identifiable by their linguistic features, and pupils need to be aware of those characteristics.
- *Statement 4* draws on the sensitivity of readers to issues, such as the density of the text, or any other linguistic features, including details such as subject–verb construction, which bring about comparative responses.
- *Statement 6* has to do with the 'sentence-level' questions pupils should have become familiar with, as a way of interrogating any familiar or previously unknown text, to begin making meaning.
- *Statement 7* is also to do with the type of response the pupil is capable of making with regard to different texts, fulfilling different purposes.

By coming to the sorts of agreements exemplified above, and by adopting the sorts of rationale and the assumptions offered by Beverley Derewianka, any English department would be creating a secure starting position for the teaching of grammatical/linguistic issues. It would also be in a better position to raise questions about progression and appropriate contexts. Having good reason to teach grammar/language understanding is one thing; making it work progressively effectively is another. It is necessary to have in place a set of outline expectations about the linguistic knowledge felt to be necessary for pupils entering Key Stage 3, and how much that knowledge will have improved by the end of the Key Stage. These sorts of decisions can be made more helpfully if departments consider how that new knowledge will have contributed to pupils becoming more fluent readers and more controlled writers.

CHAPTER 4

An Outline of the Sorts of Grammar that Pupils and Their Teachers Need to Know

> Language is central to the process of teaching and learning. Explicit knowledge about language can sharpen teachers' appreciation of children's achievements with language as well as broaden the language opportunities they provide for pupils in the classroom. It can also help teachers understand the nature of children's difficulties or partial successes with language. (Carter 1990)

It is essential in the teaching of language that pupils begin from a position that recognises their own considerable implicit knowledge of the topic. All pupils, from their regular daily familiarity with language, have some straightforward grammatical insights, but they may not have enjoyed sufficient opportunities to articulate this knowledge explicitly to themselves. In my opinion, one of the main reasons for the introduction of the Literacy Strategy at all Key Stages has been to 'make the transparent apparent'. That is, properly implemented, these strategies offer pupils the wherewithal to demonstrate that they are aware of the many interlinking but often seemingly hidden features of language that imbue it with the nuances of different meanings, fulfilling certain purposes in particular contexts.

> All teachers and pupils possess considerable knowledge about language and this knowledge has to be valued, worked with and built upon. It would also be wrong to assume that this conscious knowledge operates independently of unconscious knowledge; there is a constant interplay and interaction between different modes of knowing and explicit, analytical attention to language can and should serve to deepen intuition. (Carter 1990)

To be true explorers of this aspect of English studies, young people require a firmly based starting foundation. Pupils entering secondary school should be increasingly knowledgeable and confident about their specific linguistic insights, as the strategy takes fuller effect in Key Stages 1 and 2. Nevertheless, an excellent starting point might be to present them with a piece of text that looks, at first sight, like gibberish, but on further examination can assist with their articulation of what they instinctively know. The training materials for primary National Literacy Strategy, published in the 'lunch box' kit in 1998, contained the following passage:

> The greep dawked forily prip the blortican. It snaughted preg the melidock trippicant and shrolled nong the cretidges. Pronautically, the greep caught up with all the other dogs. They had found fresh murchin and were sprooling and muting around it. The old bradilihund was sletching his paws down the hole and the persistent chinourier had started to dig. None was sroop enough to plurt inside. The greep was not really interested; after a quick sprool he continued his journey home. The others soon abandoned the search and followed him. They were greeted by a very happy old shepherd who was sure that the dogs had been buried in the landslide. (DfEE 1998)

The passage is largely nonsense of course, but it should be the natural inclination of most people to want to impose as much meaning as possible on it. That is what many of us always seek to do with puzzling material. There are sufficient footholds in this passage to allow readers to begin that process, and as possible meanings unfold, so pupils can begin to identify more obviously how certain linguistic conventions are at work. It is as close as pupils can come to looking at language at work, as if fresh, for the first time. For a moment or two, it offers the possibility for them to be detached from the familiar, to cast an eye over words at work in a specific manner, and to apply the linguistic knowledges they have acquired through a short lifetime of familiarity.

The first thing which pupils will probably notice is that the words in the passage are divided into groups, and those groups are demarcated from other groups by marks, such as **full stops** and **commas**. All pupils should be able to offer reasons why this grouping procedure is a necessary arrangement, and also by articulating their own reasons, they should learn more than if merely being instructed to take notice of sentence structures. On at least three occasions in the passage, and seen first in the second sentence, the word 'and' is used to hold groups of words together. Where the word 'and' holds groups of words together, and does not merely act as a continuer in a list, it is called a **conjunction.**

This passage can be employed for a number of different teaching approaches. Pupils might be, first, asked to identify or suggest the **word classes** of the separate words in this context; not as an end in itself, but as a means of supplying a vocabulary for explaining how each separate word is 'at work'. By this process pupils should be able to come to the conclusion that there is a strong likelihood of the word 'greep' being seen as a **noun,** naming something, as it follows a **determiner** 'the', and that is how many nouns behave. 'Greep' also precedes a word ending with 'ed', which is probably a **verb** in the past tense, and 'greep' is acting as the **subject** of that **verb,** another characteristic of nouns. Later in the passage, two words – 'melidock trippicant' – follow the word 'the'. This collection of words is likely to be a **phrase,** as it contains no **verb** (discussed below). This point could be looked at in more detail; namely, one of those two words is probably acting as a **noun,** but there are some interesting possibilities:

- if 'trippicant' is the **noun,** then 'melidock' could be a qualifying **adjective,** adding extra meaning to its attached **noun,** as in a similar **phrase** 'the black hat';
- 'trippicant' could, however, be an **adjective,** as in the rather poetic **phrase** 'the Castle Virtuous' (although the capital letters tend to show the manner in which such phrases appear);
- both 'melidock' and 'trippicant' could be **nouns,** but one of them is acting **adjectivally** in this instance, as in 'the sandwich bar', or 'the coffee pot'.

As pupils move through the passage they will quickly recognise other, known, qualifying words, called **adjectives,** that add further meaning to nouns – '*fresh* murchin', '*old* bradilihund', '*persistent* chinourier' and '*quick* sprool' – that make the identification of naming words (**nouns**) very easy.

It should be possible to ask the pupils if they can recognise the **tense** (the time setting) of the passage. In their considerations of this topic, pupils might offer some ideas about the **purpose** of the whole passage. It is, in actual fact, not wholly meaningless! It does operate successfully, in total, as a proper text. The endings of a number of important words in the passage offer obvious clues: 'dawked', 'snaughted' and 'shrolled' are examples. As already noted, words ending in the letters 'ed' in our language usually denote that they are **verbs,** and this ending indicates that the process of this verb is complete; that the 'process' is finite. As a consequence, the passage could be described as taking place in **the past tense.** (This simple piece of knowledge, in its own right, is worth knowing for the light it throws on a small but common spelling problem. Disturbingly large numbers of pupils in Key Stage 4 still spell words such as 'shocked', 'splashed' or 'worked' as 'shockd', 'splashd' or 'workd'. Just knowing the purpose of these words, and thinking more carefully about them, could contribute to overcoming some straightforward spelling problems.) We do not yet know what the processes of 'dawking', 'snaughting' and 'shrolling' might be – but they are processes, or **verbs**, because they make sense with these characteristic endings, and act in regular ways.

A passage written in the past tense has a strong possibility of being a **recount** – a fact likely to be known by most pupils who have become experienced in thinking more closely about language as a result of their acquaintanceship with the primary Literacy Strategy. The past tense will be appropriate because the events being written about will be finished, the processes completed. A recount will need to settle its audience speedily into the situation to which it relates: Where is this event taking place? Who is there? When did it happen? This passage takes little time to let the audience know the participants, 'the greep', and we know where it was 'dawking', 'prep the blotican'. We even know how the 'dawking' was taking place: in a 'forily' manner. Recounts also move forward as narrative devices by employing connectives of time. This example does not use many of those devices but it does contain: 'after a' and 'soon'.

Some other processes are also apparent, and have similar endings: 'sprooling', 'muting' and 'sletching'. Some of these are preceded by the word 'were', and in this form are known as **verb chains,** or – slightly confusingly, but that problem occurs occasionally with language – **verb phrases**.

It is also possible to recognise other individual words, through their intrinsic characteristics, or the manner in which they are employed. 'Pronautically', for instance, ends with the letters 'ly'. Words with this ending are usually recognised as **adverbs**, and their purpose is to add further meaning to the processes of **verbs**. The **adverbs** answer 'questions' the reader can put to the text, such as 'How did the greep dawk?' Answer: 'It dawked *forily.*' The 'ly' feature is a characteristic which pupils can identify quickly on many but by no means all **adverbs** (any exceptions would then be the focus for further investigation).

In the first three sentences, the processes 'dawked', 'snaughted' and 'shrolled' are followed respectively by three words, 'prip', 'preg' and 'nong'. It is difficult, at first sight, to guess what these words might be doing. Pupils will probably have to refer to passages of English text, or other similarly structured sentences that they know well, to recognise that these words are performing the function of linking the processes of the **verbs** with the **nouns** that follow in the sentence. They help to answer such questions as 'Where did the greep dawk?' The answer: 'The greep dawked *nong* the cretidges.' We can be fairly confident that 'cretidges' is another **noun** (probably, in actual fact, a **plural noun**, because it finishes with an 's', the regular way of indicating that more than one **noun** is being mentioned) preceded as it is by another **determiner**. 'The greep dawked . . . nong the cretidges' leads us to believe that the dawking process took place 'nong' (in some proximity to) the cretidges. 'Nong the cretidges' is another **phrase** (a group of words without a **verb**), and these often begin – when answering the question 'where' – with **prepositions** (e.g. *on* the bank, *near* the farm, *under* the water).

This sort of work would make an admirable and absorbing set of starter exercises, and should offer interesting possibilities of animated discussion for a Year 7 group. They could be asked to substitute known words for those that have been made up for the passage. They might even be asked to follow up this exercise by writing a comparable passage, or – in the first instance – just a sentence of such a passage, and asked to explain what function the words are playing in their new piece. There are also real texts in the language, such as *Jabberwocky* by Lewis Carroll and *The First Men on Mercury* by Edwin Morgan, that might be chosen to illustrate that this sort of apparently 'nonsense' approach can have real validity.

Some rudimentary grammar knowledge: a 'starter kit' for teaching language

This section of the book is a particularly tricky one. Teachers will have very different levels of grammar knowledge, and background experience, so any recommendations made can be only very general. There is no ideal 'pack' of grammar with which to approach lessons, and the features that some teachers might want to emphasise will not be those selected by other colleagues. Any time spent encouraging the pupils to 'learn the parts' could also be interpreted as adopting the unfashionable practices in English lessons now long discredited.

The most helpful starting point I can suggest is to always insist that the best and most worthwhile learning will be the likeliest when these issues of linguistic identification and familiarisation take place in real textual situations. In the pages that follow every bit of information or 'knowledge' that has been offered to the readers of this book can be reworked into classroom exercises to enable pupils to *explore* the issues concerned. Teachers should be able to encourage their pupils to identify how words, phrases or clauses are at work in a variety of circumstances. Pupils should begin to gain confidence about 'the usual manner' in which language works – 'rules' are not really the best way of describing the characteristics of language, as there are so many exceptions! The best model for teachers who are teaching 'language studies' is to be ready to adopt a certain attitude ('I don't necessarily know the absolutely correct answer to that question, but how might we discover it?'). There is nothing shameful about not being the 'expert' in these circumstances.

The knowledge of the **word classes**, for instance, should never be regarded as an end in itself – it is a tool or a mechanism for being able to articulate the **functions** of what may be seen to take place in the whole range of real-life language situations. Pupils are being asked to become acquainted with the terms, or names of the different classes, so that they can put better and more searching questions to texts with increasing independence and confidence, and not just to be able to answer very limited sorts of language tests.

There have been a number of historic practices in relation to what used to be called 'parts of speech' – nowadays known more accurately as **word classes** – that need to be cleared up. The first important point that pupils need to understand and articulate for themselves is that words can be ascribed to a **word class** only when it is 'in action'. The same word can be employed in different ways in different sentences, and qualify in different classes as a consequence. The word 'running' will do as an example:

- 'the name of the activity I am undertaking is called *running*' (if it names something the word *running* at that moment is a **noun**);
- 'I am *running* as fast as I can' (in this case *running* is an activity taking place at that moment; therefore it is a **verb**);
- 'these *running* shoes stink' (this word is telling us more, and increasing our understanding of the thing that is the subject of the clause – the 'shoes'; therefore, in this context, *running* is an **adjective**).

Where pupils are asked to suggest word classes for each of these words, used differently in each context, they should be encouraged first to explore the function that word is performing.

George Keith, the linguist, has in his talks to teachers and advisers of English offered the 'map of grammar' illustrated in Figure 4.1. This simple representation of the language is a straightforward, uncomplicated starting point for teachers who are themselves learning more about the way language works. Contrary to the thinking of the Conservative government of the 1980s and 1990s, and much of the population who know little about the topic, there is not just one approach to grammar. When QCA published *The Grammar Papers* in 1998, it mentioned ten quite separate 'branches' of the subject:

- phonology – the sound system of a language;
- lexis – the total vocabulary in a language;
- morphology – the form and structure of words, their inflection, derivation and change over time;
- semantics – meaning, changes in meaning and the principles that govern

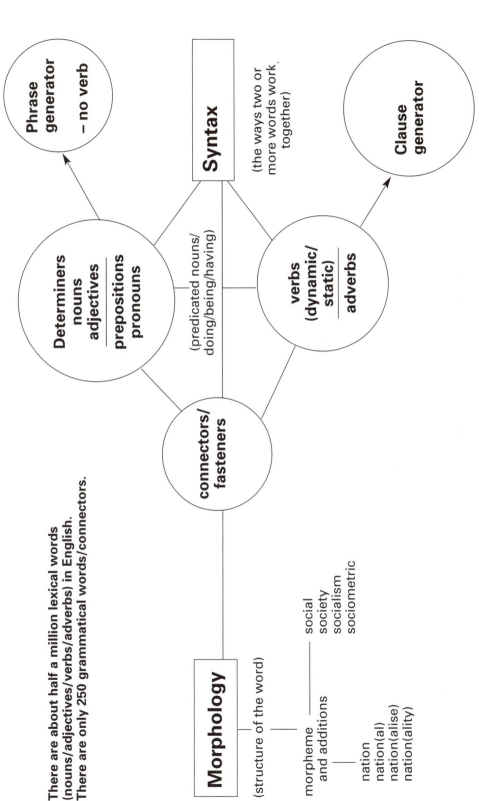

There are about half a million lexical words (nouns/adjectives/verbs/adverbs) in English. There are only 250 grammatical words/connectors.

Phrase generator – no verb

Syntax
(the ways two or more words work. together)

Clause generator

Determiners nouns adjectives prepositions pronouns

(predicated nouns/ doing/being/having)

verbs (dynamic/ static) adverbs

connectors/ fasteners

Morphology
(structure of the word)

morpheme and additions — social
society
socialism
sociometric

nation
nation(al)
nation(alise)
nation(ality)

Figure 4.1 The map of grammar (with thanks to George Keith)

the relationship between words, sentences and their meanings;
- sociolinguistics – language in relation to its social context;
- stylistics – characteristic choices in language use made by different individuals or groups;
- psycholinguistics – psychology of how language is developed and used;
- pragmatics – the interpretation of utterances in the context in which they are used;
- syntax – the combination and arrangement of words within larger structures such as phrases, clauses and sentences;
- graphology – the writing system of a language. (QCA 1998)

This is far too much for teachers and pupils to deal with, and an unnecessarily burdensome prospect. Much of this study would be either inappropriate for pupils, or – even worse – thoroughly boring; we therefore need something far more direct and manageable for classroom use.

George Keith, through the device of his 'map', foregrounds the process of text-making, and focuses on two central approaches, from which the outlines of a substantial but interesting and motivating programme of language can be constructed: **morphology** and **syntax**.

The process of text-making

The written texts of school study are about someone, something or some idea being, having or functioning in some manner, usually in **sentences** – otherwise the text would not exist. Therefore, pupils wanting to know more about how the text is functioning will want to be clear about the '**subject(s)**' of the sentences (the someone, something or some idea) – which is that portion Keith includes in the 'phrase generator'. They will also need to be able to explore what is happening, or being carried out to the subject, or what it is or has – that predicated section of the sentence (that bit included in the 'clause generator'). How the **phrases** and **clauses** relate to each other, the way in which they are capable of making meaning of different sorts in different combinations, is the stuff of grammar teaching and learning.

Morphology

Morphology is the study of structures of individual words and how alterations in structure effect (and affect) changes in meaning. Language users have a fairly large 'word hoard' at their disposal – lots of straightforward words such as 'book', 'bird', 'bag', 'bus', 'but', 'by', 'because' – all of which have independent meanings understood by the user. These everyday, no-nonsense words are called 'free morphemes'. Extra letters could be added to most of these word 'stems', but nothing can be taken away without changing their intrinsic meaning.

Adding prefixes and suffixes to these 'stem' words is called 'affixation' (the business of affixing – or adding – extra letters for particular purposes). When a **noun** is transformed into the plural form (more than one of something) it is often accomplished by affixing an 's' to indicate that this change of number has taken place – 'boy(s)'/'bag(s)'/'blouse(s)'/'beast(s)' – but sometimes (and these are the sorts of endings or sounds pupils should be exploring for themselves) we add 'es' – 'bush(es)'/'brass(es)'/'box(es)' – or even 'ies' – 'baby(ies)'/'boundary(ies)'/'bestiary(ies)'. There are, of course, other ways of indicating the shift to the plural – 'child(ren)', 'mouse' ('mice'), 'woman' ('women') – and these are also the material of independent or paired/group pupil exploration.

Other affixations might include 'ing', 'de', 'multi', 'ity', 'tion' or 'ism', depending on the function being carried out. Affixing 'ation' to a 'free morpheme', for instance, changes a **verb** to a **noun** (a process to a thing) – e.g. 'rationalise' to 'rationalisation', 'nationalise' to 'nationalisation'. (Some very helpful examples of this work are presented in the National Literacy Strategy booklet *Year 7 Spelling Bank* (DfEE 2001d), from which enterprising teachers should be able to devise some challenging exploratory morphemic activities.)

With **verb** endings, some of those features that indicate the tense are morphological affixations; the present participle indicated by 'ing' and the past participle by 'ed' in 'regular' verb past tenses are good examples. The spelling of some **verbs** can also be the same as the **noun** form – e.g. 'walking', 'waking', 'winking', 'waiting' – in fact, all those words ending in 'ing' – and a few might be employed **adjectivally** – 'walking boots', while others act as **nouns** by naming an activity (known as 'gerunds'), e.g. 'the banging of the child', 'the dripping of the tap'. Only by seeing the word 'at work' is it possible to establish the word class to which it belongs.

The planned study of morphology can contribute to pupils' spelling knowledge and understanding and to their general comprehension. Exploration of words ending in 'ence' and 'ance', 'ible' or 'able', or investigation into those words which double the middle consonant, relative to those which do not, are legitimate activities that can help pupils become more confident in attempting correct spelling. General reading comprehension can be enhanced by knowing what some 'bound morphemes' (unlike 'free morphemes', these groups of letters do not contain independent meanings) are contributing to the changed meaning of the stems to which they have been attached. George Keith offers some amusing examples of this type of work in *Learning about Language* –

Teacher's Resource (2001), where this whole topic is explained in far greater detail:

> Schlumpher – a person who schlumphs/Schlumphing – doing it schlumphed – done it/schlumphism – the belief in it schlumphist – a believer in it/schlumphology – the study of it schlumphography – writing about it/schlumpholatry – worshipping it etc. (Keith 2001)

Syntax

Syntax is the study of two or more words working together to make meaning.

In his talks, George Keith explains that:

> Grammar is about thingies doing things (or being things/or having things) – where, when and how – unto other things; or having it done unto them.

While this may not be the most intellectually challenging illumination of the topic, it does point to the vital ingredients. David Crystal (1987), however, describes it rather more simply when he writes: Grammar is about the study of sentences.'

Language is about – and would not kick into action unless – **something** (a person/thing/idea/principle/emotion) **is/was/will be involved in a process** (existing/acting out/thinking/feeling/possessing/expressing) **of some sort**. Otherwise nothing takes place, no thought is attempted, no reflection made. No language. So, a 'thingie' is always 'involved in/up to' something!

The noun group of words – the phrase generator

In English (and most other languages) a **something** is always ascribed a name – it is very necessary to be able to categorise the world into clearly distinguishable things, and to share an agreement about what those things are called. These words which perform the naming of these recognisable and separate **things** are called *nouns.*

It is helpful to think of nouns not as a single, separate 'category' of word class, but to associate them closely with the other words comprising the 'noun group' – *nouns, adjectives, determiners, pronouns* and *prepositions* – because the combination of these sorts of words leads to the construction of *phrases.*

Nouns answer the question: who? or what? is involved in any process.

Things/**nouns** can be:

- living (animal) or non-living (oil)
- human (person) or non-human (cat)
- masculine (man) or feminine (woman) or neuter (table)
- general (elephant) or particular (Jumbo)
- concrete (clock) or general (time)
- everyday (skin) or technical (epidermis)
- objective (youth) or subjective (yob)
- countable (tomatoes) or uncountable (sauce)
- common (town) or proper (Northampton)
- collective (ensemble, team)
- singular (mouse) or plural (mice)
- compound (playground, football)
- abstract (memory, honesty, subtraction, justice).

This sort of list is a useful analytical tool. It can give rise to a number of searching questions about the nature of language in different sorts of text or context. For instance, as pupils grow older they tend to be expected to learn the 'technical' names for things they may once have called by another, more common name. Maturing language use, and academic maturity, may be observed in how well pupils employ and understand 'abstract' names. The consideration of masculine, feminine or neutral names is an important stage in the way pupils perceive their world; does 'actor' or 'poet' apply to both genders, for instance, or should the term for females involved in those occupations be 'actress' and 'poetess'? Nouns that can be counted usually refer to concrete, 'real' things, while those that might be regarded as 'uncountable' are often seen to be more abstract in quality. Teachers who pay attention to these aspects of language will plan for pupils to practise and improve the sorts of questions they might put to texts about the way **nouns** have been used that can point to particular meanings.

Nouns can be created from **verbs** (processes – considered below) and **adjectives** (in this section), and pupils should be helped to see how adding **suffixes** (extra letters to the endings of words) can move the stem of a word from one function to another. For example:

- to *improve* is the intention of a process/an *improve*ment is the name of the change the process achieves;
- to *speak* is the intention of the process/a *speak*er is the name of the performer of the process;
- to *satisfy* is what is intended of the process/*satisfac*tion is the name of the intended outcome;

- *lonely* is the condition being described/*loneli*ness is the name of the condition being experienced.

The addition of the 'bound morphemes' 'ment', 'er', 'tion' and 'ness' are some of the ways that **nouns** can be easily recognised. Which other **nouns**, ending in similar ways, can pupils discover?

Pupils enjoy 'taking words for a walk' through different functions and should be given opportunities to do so:

- *child* (name of human 'thing' **noun**) – *childish* (the descriptive nature with the qualities of being a child – **adjective**) – *childishly* (how a process might be conducted in an immature manner – **adverb**). Similar examples were demonstrated in the **Morphology** section (above); for example:

  - fool/foolish/foolishly – also folly
  - significance/significant/significantly
  - worth/worthy/worthily etc.

Without, I hope, becoming too linguistically technical, it is also worth remembering that **nouns** have capabilities that are not extended to any other word class:

- they are able to be 'pluralised' – made into more than one;
- they can be possessive (in which instance they should add an apostrophe in the appropriate place – Ken's boots/the babies' prams);
- they can act as the 'headword' – the most important word – in noun phrases (e.g. 'the tiny *church* in the town').

Words which define precisely which **noun** is being referred to or talked about are called the **determiners**. Determiners include the familiar 'definite' *the* (a particular 'thingy') and 'indefinite' *a/an* (any thingy of that sort) articles – and other more or less specific words such as *this, that, those, some, few*.

This and *that* are also known as 'demonstrative pronouns' but, when taking the role of 'determining which nouns are being highlighted' they are known as *determiners* (and are acting adjectivally). Teachers and pupils should not be concerned that words may be classified into more than one group at a time. Pupils should be encouraged constantly to focus on what the *function* of the word/phrase/clause is intended to be in the particular circumstance in which it is being employed.

Adjectives are likely to be the best-known word class for most pupils. The function of the **adjective** is to add further meaning to the **noun**. It is not helpful merely to think of adjectives as 'descriptive' words – because they perform more functions than merely describing. It is also good practice to urge pupils to include the idea of the **noun** whenever the **adjective** is being talked about or explained.

Adjectives could be:

- pointing words (that, this)
- possessives (mine/their/Jane's)
- quantities (some/six)
- opinions (lonely/pretty)
- factual (blue/circular/hard/young)
- comparative (bigger/best/more)
- classifiers (*sports* shoe/*country* mouse)
- adjectival phrases – often with prepositions at the start – (the man *with the long coat*/the shop *at the end of the street*)
- adjectival clauses – (the family *living in our town*/the children *smiling across the river*).

Approaching language from a **functional** perspective might even enable teachers to tackle one of the most intractable dilemmas in all language learning. Huge numbers of pupils have very serious problems distinguishing the 's' on the end of plural nouns from the apostrophe 's' indicating possession or ownership. The *apostrophe* would probably be best taught with the possessive adjective. A possessive **noun** is, after all, acting adjectivally – offering the reader further information about the **noun** to which it is attached. Before the pupils attempt to place their apostrophe 's', they need to establish the relationship between the two juxtaposed **nouns,** for example:

- the *man's hat* – his hat – (how many men?)
- the *babies' nappies* – their nappies (how many babies?)
- a *tree's leaves* – its leaves/those *trees' leaves* – their leaves (how many trees?).

Pupils can then go on to research the 'usual practice' (insisting on grammar 'rules' is largely counter-productive because there are so many exceptions, as was mentioned earlier) in respect of:

- making a singular noun possessive by adding **'s** ('Tom's friend', 'the girl's bag', 'his mother's chair');
- adding the apostrophe to the end of plural nouns ending with 's', although this can sometimes be written as **'s** ('Mrs Jones' husband', or 'Mrs Jones's husband')

- making the regular plural noun possessive by adding the apostrophe after the 's' ('the ladies' shoes', 'the boxes' tops', 'those houses' gardens');
- making irregular plural nouns (do not usually end with 's') by adding **'s** ('the children's toys', 'these women's quarters', 'the oxen's stalls').

Then contrast the necessity of apostrophes attached to possessive nouns, to ensure the most precise meanings, with the lack of apostrophes on the possessive adjectives – 'his', 'hers', 'theirs', 'its'.

The best point from which to conduct any investigation of apostrophes is for pupils to seek them in a selection of texts of different genre; to decide from their explorations where they are most often employed, and to make a collection illustrating the range of their use – and then to extrapolate some conclusions.

Having some ideas about how **adjectival phrases** and **adjectival clauses** work and are built can offer more opportunities for constructing a wider variety of sentences. **Adjectival phrases** contain no verbs and use **prepositions** to begin a noun group. They offer more information about the **noun**, for example:

- the happiest – girl – *in all the world* (noun separated, for clarity)
- those magnificent – men – *in their flying machines*
- all the wet – men and women – *without their umbrellas*
- the biggest possible – surprise – *for the whole school.*

Adjectival clauses also offer more information about the **noun**, but they contain **verbs**, for example:

- the nation – *which* <u>fought</u> *for freedom*
- the trains – *that* <u>were speeding</u> *through the night*
- some huntsmen – <u>riding</u> *through the open countryside*
- the first men – <u>to step</u> *on the moon.*

The function of the **pronoun** is to 'substitute, or stand in for the **noun**' to allow writers to avoid using the **noun** too regularly. They also fulfil other linguistic functions such as to add emphasis. So '*Gill's* friend' can become '*her* friend', in subsequent references, or 'Linda, Paul and Andrew went *themselves* to check if it was acceptable'. **Pronouns** can be:

- personal (I/you/him)
- possessive (mine/hers/yours/theirs)
- relative (which/that/who/whom)
- questioning (who?/what?)

- emphasising (himself/yourself/themselves/itself).

The verb group of words – the clause generator

Verbs are the powerhouse of our language, enabling the 'thingies' to 'get up to something' or to 'be or have'. In any text on grammar more space is rightly afforded to the consideration of verbs than any other word class, because the verbs perform so many functions. For these reasons it is *not* a helpful description to term **verbs** merely as 'doing words', which teachers have persisted in doing for too long. This definition is too constraining and precludes all the other jobs that verbs perform. They can be 'doing' words – but as more verbs are formed around the notions of 'being' and 'having' in the majority of written texts, that title can be very misleading.

When we are interested in how language functions to represent the world, we look at how different types of verbs are involved in expressing different aspects of our experience:

- action verbs
- saying verbs
- sensing verbs (e.g. thinking, feeling, perceiving verbs)
- relating verbs. (Derewianka 1998)

There is almost too much for pupils to know about **verbs**, certainly requiring far more space than is available here, but a few central features can be extremely supportive for potential writers. One of the great difficulties about studying grammar and language is that so often the different concepts are overlapping and interdependent.

> You can't understand what a finite verb is until you have a notion of subject agent and tense; you can't understand gerunds until you know about verb participles; you know what an adverb is because you know it isn't an adjective, and so on. (Keith 2001)

Verbs have the capacity to indicate to a reader (or listener) the 'person(s)' of any activity/process – that is, who is featured, and the 'tense' (time) in which the activity or process takes place.

Knowing the difference between 'finite' and 'infinitive' **verbs** is an important distinction.

- *Infinitive **verbs*** are the base or central stem from which the rest of the **verb** develops. They can be recognised by the word *to* which precedes them (e.g. *to* be, *to* go, *to* understand, *to* skip, *to* administrate). In that stage they have no 'person', no 'tense', because they have not been to work in relationship with a 'something' at any time.

Pupils need to know that the vital words 'is', 'was' and 'were' derive from the infinitive form 'to be'; or that 'went' is derived from the infinitive 'to go', and 'had' belongs to 'to have'.

- *finite verbs* are verbs in action – and usually indicate to us by their endings *who* is involved in the activity/process, and *when* it is being played out.

The 'who' bit of sentences can sometimes give rise to problems in Standard English for pupils, particularly where the local dialect supports spoken constructions that are not acceptable in written language (e.g. 'we was', 'they was') when the expected plural construction would usually be 'we were'/'they were'. Pupils need to see how these constructions come about – and realise that they should be applied in their own writing, whatever may be acceptable in the way they naturally speak.

Another interesting puzzle to discuss in relation to **verbs**, capable of providing the material of worthwhile classroom exploration, is concerned with whether they can be attributed the categories of 'regular' or 'irregular'. Pupils have little trouble discerning between them – the 'bound morpheme' 'ed', when attached to most regular **verbs,** indicates that whatever is taking place is in the past (e.g. stopped, grated, finished, waned, waited, crossed).

Irregular **verbs** use a whole range of endings to indicate time past (e.g. ran, swam, bit, spoke, swore, spat, flew). These endings are referred to as 'past participles'. Many pupils encounter real difficulties in maintaining consistent tenses throughout their work, and may start to write a passage in the past tense, but then drift into the present, when writing without sufficient care and attention.

An interesting feature of **verb** use – lending itself to further pupil study, as it is not always confidently understood by weaker language users – is that the work of **verbs** can often involve more than one word. Indeed, they can occasionally be up to five separate, but related, words all concerned with the functions of the verb (e.g. 'need not have been cheating') where 'cheating' is the main part of the **verb**. More usually, however, **verbs** are expressed in groups of two or three words (e.g. has been, was going, had finished, is happening, will be talking). These groups of words, performing the functions of putting the 'subjects' into some form of activity or existence, are confusingly known as **verb phrases**, or sometimes **verb chains**.

Verb phrases are constructed by calling on a subgroup of **verbs**, 'auxiliaries' (e.g. 'to be', 'to have'), or 'modal auxiliaries' (e.g. 'can', 'could', 'may', 'might', 'will', 'would', 'shall', 'should'). These extra features of **verbs** give speakers and writers far more opportunities to develop the meanings of the **main verbs**, and therefore to write with greater sensitivity and focus. Pupils should (there's an example of a 'modal' at work straight away!) be asked to consider and explain the differences between groups of words such as:

- I talk/I am talking/I might talk/I should talk/I can talk/I have been talking/I was talking/I will be talking/I would be talking, etc.

The main **verb** word that carries most of the meaning in these **verb phrases** clearly derives from the infinitive root 'to talk', but the 'auxiliaries' and 'modals' have added so much more to the audience's understanding of the speaker's/writer's time frame and intentions.

Occasionally, a writer will break up a **verb chain**, to give greater emphasis to what has been stated (e.g. I was only just starting) where 'was . . . starting' is the **verb chain,** and 'only' and 'just' have been inserted to give an exact sense of when the 'starting' took place. The words 'only' and 'just' are modifying the idea of 'starting', answering the question 'when was the starting?'; thus they are acting **adverbially**. This paragraph should also be alerting aware language users to another characteristic of **verbs**. In the **verb chain** 'I was only just starting', 'starting' is a **verb,** but prior to that I wrote of '*the* starting', where 'starting' is obviously preceded by 'the' – a **determiner. Determiners,** as has already been explored, work to assist the meanings of **nouns,** so in this instance a **verb** has miraculously become a **noun,** and is known as a 'gerund'. Many **verbs** ending in 'ing' can be 'transferred' from one situation to another – they could be words denoting the action or process continuing to take place, or the name of the activity or process. **Verbs** have this capability of becoming **nouns** and **adjectives,** depending on *how* the word is expected to be functioning – and that phenomenon happens a great deal in mainstream language use. Teachers could devise exercises that would enable pupils to recognise the difference between these words, depending on their role in any stated part in a phrase, clause or sentence; for example, spot the difference between and explain what is happening in the following:

- 'the dam *burst* dramatically' vs. 'the *burst* balloon' or 'the wheel was *spinning*' vs. 'the *spinning* wheel'.
- 'the car is *turning* in a circle' vs. 'the *turning* was a tricky manoeuvre'; 'he was *chewing* gum' vs. 'stop that *chewing*!'

The final consideration to be raised about **verbs** in this section – and there are many others that could be studied, but those characteristics are likely to emerge out of the starter suggestions already offered – is that finite **verbs** can be thought of in the 'active voice' or the 'passive voice'. Subjects of sentences are either performing the action or receiving it. Most writing is set out in the 'active voice', but there are contexts when 'passivisation' (adding 'isation' to the end of an **adjective** has created a **noun**) is appropriate and necessary. Victims of some upsetting situations learn quickly that moving into the 'passive voice' is an effective way of representing their case. Compare the difference between:

- 'I broke the glass' vs. 'The glass was broken'.

But those in authority can often employ passivisation for their own ends too! Compare:

- 'I noticed. . .' vs. 'It has been brought to my notice. . .'.

The effect is impersonal and distanced, and is employed regularly by the writers of newspaper headlines to urge the reader to pay attention to a particular group, as in:

- 'Mayor condemns vandals'

which might be transformed more powerfully into:

- 'Vandals condemned by Mayor'.

More assured writers need to be able to call on the passive voice to make arguments or to detach themselves from issues in certain contexts and subjects. Knowing how to call on this aspect of the writing repertoire is a skill that pupils can benefit from considerably, and only by enabling their classes to recognise, practise and challenge this issue will teachers ensure that progress is made.

There are considerable numbers of words that add something extra to **verbs,** or modify their meanings in some way, and these are known as **adverbs**. Pupils will mostly recognise some of these words, in the first instance, by their 'ly' endings (e.g. quickly, firmly, wildly, happily); although this quick clue by no means applies to all adverbs (e.g. as, when, just, so). What most pupils are unaware of, and should be enlightened about through some directed teaching, is that **adverbs** also modify or 'intensify' the power of adjectives (e.g. very, quite, exceptionally – to 'intensify' adjectives as in '*very* stupid', '*quite* dull' and '*exceptionally* dense').

Adverbs or **adverbials** (the name given to phrases doing the work of adverbs) are used frequently to add more to the meanings of **verbs**, by making clearer *when*, *where* or *how* the action or process of the verb took place. They answer imaginary questions the audience of a piece of text might put, for example:

- 'When did that happen?' – **adverbial** of time;
- 'Where did that happen?' – **adverbial** of place;
- 'How did that happen?' – **adverbial** of manner.

These imaginary questions can sometimes be answered as single words, or they can be structured in phrases, and careful writers will need to be aware of the possibility of different effects brought about by the use of both alternatives in appropriate contexts; for example:

- 'They left the town *yesterday*' or 'they left the town *as the sun rose*'; 'the boots were lined up *outside*' or 'the boots were lined up *alongside the shed*'; 'I answered their questions *cheerfully*' or 'I answered their questions *with a cheerful and amused attitude*'.

One of the great advantages about being aware of the flexibility of adverbials is that writers are then able to use them in different parts of sentences for particular effects. They could start the sentence (usually in the 'ly' ending form):

- *Reluctantly*, she decided to tell him the truth.

Adverbials can also be inserted part way through the sentence for particular emphasis:

- I moved, *slowly and deliberately*, towards the edge.

Or they can be placed at the end of the sentence:

- The whole group enjoyed themselves *throughout the entire evening*.

Pupils could discuss the differences in meaning brought about by deciding where to place the **adverbial phrase**:

- *Reluctantly*, she decided to tell him the truth.
- She *reluctantly* decided to tell him the truth.
- She decided, *reluctantly*, to tell him the truth.
- She decided to tell him the truth *reluctantly*.

An area of linguistic knowledge which has been given far more attention since the introduction of the National Literacy Strategy is the study and understanding of **connectives**. With a sharper focus being applied to the conscious use of genres in pupils' writing there has been a recognition of how particular text types are 'held together', because those **connectives** are functioning in very clear, contextual ways. Thus, a 'recount' text may be running through the events comprising an experience of some sort, and will depend on connectives of time to enable the reader to follow the sequence of those events (e.g. 'next', 'later', 'afterwards', 'at twenty past six', 'when they had finished'). An 'explanatory' text will attempt to make the causal relationships of participants or the various agents in a phenomenon clear to the audience, and will depend on such words or phrases as 'hence', 'accordingly', 'as a result of . . .', 'if . . . is added to . . ., then the consequence will be . . .', 'because of . . . so . . . will happen', or 'it may happen that . . .', etc. The non-chronological or information text will be held together by sequential features (e.g. 'first', 'followed by'); comparative characteristics (e.g. 'when compared with', 'similarly'); and causal links (e.g. 'when . . ., then . . .', 'because of . . .'). Sometimes these connectives will be single words, known as **conjunctions** – 'and', 'but', 'so', 'although' – but they will often be the sorts of phrases illustrated in this paragraph.

Left until last, yet possibly the topics that should have been dealt with first because of their vital importance, are the references to **phrases, clauses** and **sentences**.

> Most of my group of Lang/Lit students, about to take their exams, arrived with scant knowledge of the difference between verbs, nouns, adjectives or pronouns and no knowledge at all of how sentences are composed of phrases and clauses. (Clarifying this, incidentally, was a big help in sorting out some students' difficulties in constructing complete sentences and knowing how to punctuate them accurately, a problem that had hung over them through KS3 and KS4.) (Bleiman 1999)

From the preceding material in this chapter, readers should have concluded that if language is to be seen effectively at work, it is generally brought together and contained in **sentences** – units of language capable of full meaning in their own right. The usual expectation of sentences is that they will contain a finite **verb**; that is, one that is in action, or existing, in time and about a subject(s) of some sort. The part that contains the subject, and no finite verb, is usually referred to as the **phrase**. **Phrases** offer a lot of fun for classroom study. Pupils will not necessarily realise that phrases have to fulfil the criteria I offered in the previous sentence – and usually will think of a **phrase** as being made up of only two or three words. The following development example (easily adapted for classroom use) can help to consolidate the proper understanding of this feature:

- The bun. . .
- The brown bun. . .
- The brown currant bun. . .
- The brown, stale, cinnamon and currant bun in the baker's. . .
- The brown, stale, cinnamon and currant bun in the window of the baker's shop at the bottom of the High Street, near the roundabout beside the school. . .

Every one of those groups of words is a **phrase** – in this example a **noun phrase**. All these words are adding to the idea of 'bun'. At no point did the 'bun' get up to anything or get acted upon – such as *being sold, eaten, crumbled* and *thrown* to the ducks! The phrase was merely expanded by adding **determiners, nouns, adjectives** and **prepositions** to offer more specific information about the 'subject' of the sentence – a bun. Being able to build phrases in this manner gives writers more room for manoeuvre and means they can build ideas in much more detailed ways. **Adjectival phrases** and **adverbial phrases** are ways of constructing groups of words capable of standing in for, or performing the functions of **adjectives** or **adverbs** respectively. A number of examples of both sorts of phrase are given earlier in this chapter.

Clauses are the central concern of **sentences**. They are the parts, containing a finite **verb**, ensuring the subject is 'predicated' – in action or existence. 'Independent clauses' are the same as 'simple sentences'.

- 'The man' is a **phrase** – 'The man laughed', or 'The man laughs', or 'The man is laughing', 'The man might have been laughing'.

These are all **clauses**, because the original **phrase** has now been activated in each case – and they all make complete sense in their own right. 'Dependent clauses' are clauses that are unable to stand alone, as there is too little information in them to make complete sense; they might well contain a finite **verb**, but that is not enough:

- 'because they were too tired', or 'when the game finished', or 'in the garden behind the big wall'.

These clauses answer the sorts of questions a reader might raise to determine more about 'why?', 'when?' or 'where?' something occurred – but none of them inform the reader of what that occurrence might have been.

Pupils really do gain in power and control of their written work if they are confident about knowing the difference between:

- A single, independent clause – 'Some people walked through the yard', which is known as a 'simple sentence'.
- Two or more independent clauses, joined together by **conjunctions** such as 'and' or 'but' – 'Five children appeared *and* marched boldly up to the Inspector'. This is known as a 'compound sentence' (both parts are equally independent, both parts have the same authority, but they are a more efficient and quick way of moving through the matter being written about). In this example, they also make it unnecessary to repeat the subject of both sentences, namely 'five children'.
- At least one independent clause attached to one or more dependent clauses by **conjunctions** or **connectives** – 'The team struggled to keep together *because* their best player was injured' – known as 'complex sentences'.

In all the examples I have used in this section, I have deliberately chosen to employ sentences (and clauses) constructed in a **subject–verb** order. Much writing in English – about 90 per cent – is based on this pattern. It is easy for pupils to remember the letters 'SV' to denote this order. Looking for the SV order is a very useful and powerful tool for reading analysis and may be used by teachers to ask pupils to suggest other ways of constructing sentences. Pupils who grow more confident with this method of self-analysis could be introduced to other abbreviations representing 'chunks' of sentences for their own use. The following ideas, from *A Grammar of Contemporary English* by Quirk *et al.* (1972), should interest most Key Stage 3 pupils and be used by them at some point (a few might even have done some preliminary work on this topic in Key Stage 2):

S – subject (a single noun or noun phrase);
V – verb (single word or verb chain);
O – object (single word or phrase);
A – adverbial (word or phrase telling us how, when, where, why something occurred);
C – complement (something added to inform us more about the subject or object of the verb, often used with 'to be').
e.g. A pig flew. (SV) A pink headstrong pig flew last night. (SVA) An exhausted pig was flying very badly. (SVA) That pig flying to Rome was very exhausted. (SVAVC) Flying badly, the pig altered course to enable a shorter flight. (VSVOA)

Awareness of these constructional 'parts' can help pupils to think more about their own choices and consider the varieties of sentences they read and attempt to write in many contexts. Such knowledge also makes them more alive to the relationship of the different parts of sentences.

Before concluding anything on sentences, however, it is necessary to ensure that certain fundamental principles of sentences are well understood. All sentences may be categorised as:

- *statements* – declaratives, stating some idea, usually based on the SVO order;
- *questions* – interrogatives, where the usual sentence order is changed to make an enquiry, often opened by the 'wh' words (who, why, when, etc.), but also constructed in other ways worth exploring;
- *commands* – imperatives, formed by omitting the subject, or by using 'let' or 'do';
- *exclamations* – placing an emphasis on an idea or particular feature, sometimes introduced by 'what' or 'how', not used as question words.

This chapter was never meant to be an exhaustive or definitive guide to grammar. It has done little more than scratch the surface of a monumental topic. Yet teachers have to start somewhere, and these suggestions offer a sound foothold for further classroom consideration. Raising some of the issues recommended in this section will, in turn, lead on to further areas of exploration as required. Glossaries of necessary terms and meanings used throughout this chapter are available in many of the resources listed at the end of this book.

CHAPTER 5

Using Grammar to Improve Reading

Allied to this emphasis on description and analysis rather than evaluation, is the fact that the range and scope offered by linguistic study is almost limitless. Any fragment of language in use is a valid object of study, from an ansaphone message left by a council employee to a mailshot or an estate agent's blurb. The curriculum is expansive and open as compared with the pitifully constrained curriculum on offer these days in Literature courses. (Bleiman 1999)

In most of the research findings and documentation consulted in the writing of this book, the study of grammar has usually been referred to in relation to the improvement of writing. Rarely, if ever, is it considered in relation to impacting upon pupils' reading attainment. Thus for many teachers there is a likelihood that attention to grammar has not been used much in the classroom to assist the reading process. This is not a surprising finding. Teachers of English have traditionally focused their pupils' attention on the themes of fiction texts read in the classroom, with discussion and interest centred on character, plot and setting. Pupils have often been required to make a personal response in an evaluative rather than a descriptive manner. Particular features of the written style and certain notable effects might be foregrounded in certain study, but strict attention to the language of the text is often the most neglected area. The reasons for this reticence have possibly been that many teachers have not been confident about their own linguistic knowledge, and some may have believed that paying attention to such details might spoil the relationship between author and reader, and, ultimately, the 'enjoyment' of the text. This book intends to offer ways of showing how that relationship can be positively enhanced by making the language of the text a central issue of investigation.

One of the vital tasks of any English teacher should be to enable his or her pupils to make ready and open-minded relationships with new and unfamiliar texts they encounter in a wide variety of contexts. The making of meaning is a primary concern of the subject. A central intention of the teaching of reading must be to give young people the confidence, and to develop sufficient interest, for them to want to dig deeper into the meanings of all texts. With proper practice they should, when introduced to texts of which they have no previous experience, become sufficiently prepared to demonstrate that same willingness to readily engage as a way of discovering how meanings are being made in that new instance. Only by overtly tackling such issues in the classroom can teachers assist their pupils to become ready responders with and better choosers of texts in the future.

One way of supporting pupils in forming relationships with unfamiliar texts is to help them devise a repertoire of linguistic enquiries to use independently in such encounters. This way of working with texts has been explained and promoted by a range of different researchers, academics and writers concerned with the teaching of English for many years, but, for the reasons explained in Chapter 1, has never been formulated into coherent teaching practice. The LINC project, for instance, exploring language-based teaching in English classrooms between 1989 and 1992, produced a set of *Materials for Professional Development* (1992), containing a chapter 'Reading the World' which included 'A framework for looking at texts' (see Box 5.1). The first two questions – 'Who speaks this text?' and 'Who is being spoken to?' – are concerned very much with issues of language. At the foot of the page are the four areas of the textual 'evidence base' ('the detailed *rhetorical choices* which writers make'), from which a conclusion and judgements about the main questions can be made. The 'grammatical' evidence is regarded as most necessary in this process of making meaning.

In Chapter 3 I described the possible desirable 'qualities' in the reader which English departments might want to promote, including the following:

1. A reader knows that reading is a complex, intellectual endeavour, requiring the reader to draw on a range of active meaning-making skills.
3. A reader is aware that texts are constructed for particular purposes, for identifiable audiences and within recognisable text types or genres.
6. A reader is able to activate a growing repertoire of critical and analytical questions in engagements with new and unfamiliar texts.
7. A reader knows increasingly how to interact appropriately with a variety of text types/genres for particular purposes.

Not one of these 'qualities' actually mentions the words 'grammar' or 'language', but those highlighted here are strongly connected with linguistic insights and knowledge.

Statement 1 is about pupils being aware, on a number of fronts as they read texts, that meaning can be discovered through many different

Box 5.1 A framework for looking at texts

---

1. WHO SPEAKS THIS TEXT?

Is there an 'I' or a 'we' in the text? What kind of voice is this? Does the writer address me directly, or through an adopted 'persona'?

2. WHO IS BEING SPOKEN TO?

Is there a 'you' in the text? What kind of audience is being addressed, and how can we tell? Am I prepared to include myself in this audience?

3. WHERE DOES THIS TEXT COME FROM?

What do we know about when, why and how it was produced? Does the text itself disclose these things? What status does it have? What values does the text assume?

4. WHAT KIND OF TEXT IS THIS?

What other texts does it remind me of? What form does it take? What recognisable conventions has the writer adopted?

5. WHAT DOES THE TEXT WANT?

What do I deduce about the writer's intentions? Are these intentions openly stated? What kind of reading does this text invite?

6. WHAT DOES THIS TEXT MEAN TO ME?

What are my motives as a reader of this text? How have I chosen to interpret it? Do I share its values? What thoughts has it prompted?

You might like to ask all these questions of the page you are holding. . .

The resources of written texts

In discussing these questions, it might be helpful to consider some detailed *rhetorical choices* which writers make:

- **PRESENTATIONAL: e.g. choices of lay-out, typeface, illustration.**
- **ORGANISATIONAL: e.g. choices of narrative, logical, metrical or figurative pattern.**
- **GRAMMATICAL: e.g. choices of tense, mode, person, syntax, punctuation.**
- **LEXICAL: e.g. choices of vocabulary, idiom, metaphor.**

Source: LINC (1992)

approaches – including an awareness of language. The real point of this 'reading knowledge' is that pupils are actively searching for ways into meaning. Statement 3 recognises openly that texts fall into recognisable genres, and that these genres are established because of their purposefully linguistic structurings. Pupils who know that texts serve understood purposes will become increasingly familiar with the patterns or devices that serve those purposes. Statement 6 is concerned with pupils being taught to run through an intellectual repertoire of questions, including – with high priority – those about the language of the text when approaching unfamiliar material. Statement 7 is about teaching readers to recognise which features of the text to deal with in any sort of meaning-making pursuit, depending on the reading circumstance. Knowing that it could be advantageous, for instance, to identify certain linguistic characteristics is a further learning goal in the broad view of reading from which these statements are taken.

Appendix 8.1 of the 'Reading' section of the 'English Department Training 2001' (DfEE 2001c) contains a collection of exemplar 'text-level', 'sentence-level' and 'word-level' prompts that I contributed to 'frame' the sorts of questions teachers might put to their classes in shared and guided reading contexts. These are by no means the only questions confident readers might put to texts, but they offer a model of a particular approach that teachers could adopt and extend. The text-level examples include such considerations as:

- What is my major purpose in reading this text?
- What can I immediately begin to understand?
- Why has my teacher asked me to engage with this text?
- What do I know about these sorts of texts?
- What sort of support might help me become a more independent reader of this text? (DfEE 2001c)

There is also a set of 'word-level' prompts; for example:

- Is the vocabulary of this text mostly familiar, or are some words unfamiliar?
- Is the vocabulary consistent, or do changes occur at different times (and can I explain those changes)?
- Is it possible to ascertain the intended audience of the text from the sorts of words being used?
- Are certain words/phrases/ideas highlighted or emphasised for special reasons (can I determine what those reasons are)? (*ibid.*)

Sentence-level questions

More pertinent to the subject of this book are the 'sentence-level' questions, or linguistically focused issues, that teachers will want their pupils to practise and, in time, formulate for themselves. It is important to note that these questions have been devised to be put to any sort of text and not exclusively fiction narrative. Typical 'sentence-level' prompts (and their implications) might be:

- What is immediately noticeable about the layout/presentation of this text, and what might that information tell me about the meaning?
  Pupils could be guided to explore whether the book is in chapters, or arranged in other ways. They could be asking about whether the text is set in continuous prose, in sentences and paragraphs – or in bullet points, or even verse. What sorts of meaning might be immediately deduced from this sort of information?

- How dense/straightforward is this text? Does it use metaphorical/ difficult/accessible language?
  An uncomplicated set of questions. The use of figurative language can be a serious obstruction for the further reading of some less confident readers. Establishing the nature of the problem is a useful starting point in attempting to address it.

- What is the average sentence length? Do the sentence lengths vary, or are they consistent? What do these facts help me understand? What effects do they create?
  This is a crucial approach, and one that all readers – of whatever ability – can begin to adopt at an early stage of reading. Published texts in particular are mature pieces of work, constructed by adults and undergoing careful editing processes. Writers mean what they write – and the manner in which that writing was constructed. Enormous insights into meaning can often be made by detecting the contrast between long, short and medium-length sentences. The example of Keats' poem Ozymandias, considered below, is very notable. Readers are also able to begin making some judgements about the age of a text from the relative lengths of sentences. This should not be a mechanical practice – counting is not a characteristic English 'exercise'! The real point of carrying out such an activity is to draw conclusions and posit theories about the possible authorial intentions discovered from it.
  Pupils also need to be aware of how the structure of texts has changed over the years; reading today is often a very different experience from what it was in the mid-nineteenth century. They could be encouraged to

select half a dozen texts from the later part of the Victorian period, half a dozen from the mid-twentieth century, and a similar number of contemporary texts. Can they detect any differences in the average length of sentence among the texts from each period? Are there any differences in the use of punctuation from period to period? What conclusions can pupils draw about the relative ease of reading of these texts, and what might these findings suggest about general changes in language?

NB: This sort of activity is often the first successful stage of engagement for reluctant readers, a high proportion of whom are boys.

- Are most of the sentences statements, or are other sentence types also regularly used? How and why?

  It is usual to find that most sentences in prose are statements, but there are alternatives. A text beginning with a number of questions, for instance, should attract particular interest, as would exclamations or commands. They would require some investigation, and the answers would contribute to further meaning-making.

- Are there any special effects in the language which the author uses for particular purposes?

  The opening of Peter Dickinson's novel Eva *(1988) begins with unfinished sentences – really no more than phrases – in italics. He intends the reader to assume that the central character is in a drugged/dream state. Similar examples may be found in many texts.*

- Is the language use typical of known text types or genres?

  Text types are examples of genres, but text types will often integrate different genres. It is not unusual to come across examples of persuasive argument, or narrative recount, or discursive explanation. Thus readers may well be seeking typical structurings or effects associated with particular genres, as well as being aware of overlapping genre. Sometimes the intrusion of uncharacteristic or unexpected genre will be discernible – and readers might, through explaining those juxtapositions, be focusing more clearly on meaning.

- Does the writer break any conventions and what is the effect?

  Much of our reading is settled and comfortable, and we can depend on texts unfolding and developing in predictable ways. Occasionally the author will surprise or even challenge the reader. Robert Swindells in Stone Cold *(1993) employs two separate converging first-person narratives that indicate two separate characters moving closer towards a dramatic ending, creating a strong sense of suspense. The opening of* Martin Farrell *by Janni Howker (1994) presages a distinctive dialect linguistic construction, giving greater intensity to the narrative: 'This man, he had no sort of name to waste breath on, he filled his mouth with drink.'*

- Are there any recognisable patterns or structures in the language?
  Some school textbooks are constructed on clearly patterned sentences and paragraphs. Much of the meaning of many poems is almost wholly dependent on the reader discovering patterns. Lemony Snickert in his comic series of texts A Series of Unfortunate Events *is regularly able to create amusing moments by repetition: 'The particular knot she was using was called the Devil's Tongue. A group of female Finnish pirates invented it back in the fifteenth century, and named it the Devil's Tongue because it twisted this way and that, in the most complicated and eerie way. The Devil's Tongue was a very useful knot' (Snickert 1999).*

- Who is the narrator/teller of this text?
  This consideration is a vital first step in establishing the possible meanings in texts. Authors of fiction can choose whether to 'frame' the narrative from a single individual's perspective – such as the two first-person narrators of Berlie Doherty's Dear Nobody *(1991), who share very personal, intimate reflections on the events taking place; or the contrast of the Snicket (1999) approach, where the author may adopt an expansive, omniscient overview of events – and comment on them.*

- What is the tone or approach of this text? Is it consistent or does it change for special reasons?
  Textbooks are usually distant and authoritative, while novels can be intimate and colloquial. It would be unusual to find those two expectations reversed, but degrees of formality and informality are used by authors for various purposes. Understanding the tone of poetry is vital in beginning to gain an insight into the possible meanings.

- How does the style influence my reading, understanding and appreciation of the text?
  Ultimately, teachers will want their pupils to make an evaluation of what they are reading; to contrast the style of the current text with other texts. Pupils should be called to account and required to explain the styles they find most engaging most quickly, partly to contribute to better understanding of reading knowledge, and partly to articulate the points of departure for reading development.

There is nothing mechanical and distant about being able to call on and employ these questions (and others like them that teachers might want to devise) in relation to the learning of reading. They all, however, require a background of language knowledge – or some degree of grammar. They are all ways of 'holding texts up to the light' and asking robust questions about them. Some of the questions can be answered at a straightforward, unsophisticated level, and would enable the least confident readers to make further progress in their reading endeavours. Others can be pursued at a deeper level of understanding, and would be more appropriate for able readers. The most able should be encouraged to devise questions of this nature for themselves or other class members to put to the texts being studied.

Close reading techniques: using grammar knowledge

In *Teaching Reading in Secondary Schools* (Dean 2000), I demonstrated a technique of reading with pupils in classrooms – either as a whole-class activity or in a guided session – intended to enable pupils to pay particular attention to the language and other available means that might assist recognition of the structural decisions being made by the author. I have borrowed and developed this technique from George Keith, who first published this approach in his valuable chapter 'Noticing grammar' in the QCA publication *Not Whether But How* (QCA 1999). The chapter is prefaced with the following rationale:

> The chapter illustrates the argument . . . that analysis is the key feature in the development of explicit knowledge of language structure. Central to the routine discussion of language he describes what he refers to as 'noticing'. Noticing features of language whilst engaged in reading, writing or talking, whether planned for by the teacher or arising spontaneously in pupil comment, is the start of the process of making implicit grammatical knowledge explicit. To explain the function of particular linguistic features or patterns that have been noticed, or to account for their effect on readers or listeners, the features will have to be named. (QCA 1999)

'Noticing grammar' can be used in a number of ways, but it is most strongly recommended as the way a text may be introduced initially to a class or group, and then it can be used occasionally to review the text at a later stage of reading. This activity could be conducted with copies of the original text but it is also a good idea to photocopy the first page (or two) so that the pupils have none of the other clues that might normally accompany the introduction of a text, such as the cover of the book and its blurb. A photocopied piece of text also allows pupils to undertake text marking as a way of making direct contact. The pupils should cover up all the written text except – at most – the first sentence. They are then expected to pay close attention to each *word* as it is revealed, attempting to explain what function or part it is playing in the sentence. Part of the point of the exercise is to explain why the author may have chosen that particular word or construction, given that there are almost limitless other possibilities from which to choose.

In *Teaching Reading in Secondary Schools* (Dean 2000) I modelled this activity using Lesley Howarth's *Maphead* (1994), Peter Dickinson's *Eva* (1988) and Terry Pratchett's *Truckers* (1989). In *Teaching English in the Key Stage 3 Literacy Strategy* (Dean 2002) I conducted the same activity, but with Louis Sacher's popular novel *Holes* (1998). Here, I will undertake the same exercise with two very contrasting books, Jan Mark's vivid and realistic *heathrow nights* (2000) and Theresa Breslin's harrowing and finely perceived novel of class differences, yet a picture of universal suffering in the First World War, *Remembrance* (2002).

I want to make it clear that this method is an occasional activity. It is not meant to be a 'test' situation in any respect, requiring pupils to show that they have learned 'the naming of parts'. There is no need for pupils to actually be able to use such terms as 'modals' or 'modifying adverbs', but the more accurate the terms they can employ, the more specific might be their understanding. It is a very helpful way of introducing a novel to a class, but would not be used for many parallel lessons. The teacher would always want pupils to be aware of the broader unfolding of the narrative as soon as possible, and it is necessary to regard the text as a *whole*. Used sparingly, however, this strategy can be genuinely powerful, and has the capability of engaging pupils very quickly in the tone, intention, purpose and full meaning of the text.

heathrow nights begins with the following paragraph:

One

We intercepted the letters. I don't know if the others read theirs, I opened mine standing there in the hall, with the rest of the envelopes on the carpet, fanned out, face down, just as they had been when they landed. With a criminal instinct I didn't know I possessed I'd marked all their positions before I scooped them up, picked out mine and put them back again.

Only it wasn't mine. (Mark 2000)

The first piece of information on the page is the word 'one' set in the middle of the page. On this occasion it indicates the number of the chapter, no more (and may be checked by referring to the rest of the book, and discovering that the next section is headed by 'two', the next 'three' and so on). In some books this heading might be more informative. It might be:

'Day One', or 'Preface', or 'The way this story begins' – all of which would signify different ways of approaching the contents and searching for some early meanings.

The first sentence is four words long. Short sentences have an obvious potential for focusing meaning in a very limited space. 'We' has two effects – it informs the reader that there will be a first-person narrator (so the events will be observed from a particular viewpoint), and it points to more people being involved in the narration at this point than the protagonist. The main process of the sentence – the verb 'intercepted' – suggests an underhand, not wholly honest act. Whoever should have received the object of the sentence, 'the letters' (and we know absolutely nothing about these 'letters' at this point, except that the protagonist does not want an unknown 'them' to see their contents) has been prevented from doing so. There is an indication that something not wholly legitimate is being described.

The second sentence contrasts strongly with the first. It is 37 words long; very lengthy for a modern sentence. It is more expansive and developed than the first, tight statement. This one begins not with 'we', but 'I'. This standing apart from the 'others' is a point of interest at this stage. The protagonist 'doesn't know' – a contraction, typical of normal speech patterns, expected of the first-person narrator, and informing us that he is unaware of the behaviour of the others to whom 'I' was attached from the start. The second clause of the sentence is really another sentence in its own right, but the author bundles a series of clauses together as an explanation, with lots of detail packed together – 'fanned out, face down' – to contrast with the protagonist reading the letter that has been selected from the rest. Active processes (verbs) are emphasised heavily in this passage: 'opened', 'marked', 'scooped', 'picked' and 'put' suggest a great deal of animation. The pronoun 'I' becomes very significant in this paragraph. It appears in sentences two and three, and then as the conclusion of the very short fourth sentence, drawing much attention to itself through its repetition and its position. This attention is made more acute as this sentence stands alone in its paragraph.

The possessive pronoun 'mine' is clearly important, and there is a suggestion that the protagonist has some strong claim on these letters, but there is a realisation that they actually belong to someone else, confirming the phrase 'a criminal instinct'. This 'is it mine/is it not mine?' dilemma establishes an early tension in the narrative.

The first part of the story has built up a tension ('mine/not mine'); set up an intriguing possibility for readers to explore ('criminal instinct'); indicated that this story is likely to be based on action (many active processes) and has foregrounded a first-person narrator who is somehow in league with as yet unknown other people, but who maintains an independence from them. These are essential developmental features to bear in mind at this stage of the novel (and will prove to be important pointers to what will actually take place in the rest of the story). The use of 'I', by the way, without any immediate revelation as to the identity of that character, is a very old method of setting up an interest in the reader who wants to discover to whom reference is being made.

The second paragraph begins:

> I started to take it out of the envelope addressed to Mrs S. Jagger, with the school's name printed along the top, the school having not yet caught up with the fact that she is no longer Mrs S. Jagger but Mrs S. Hague. The school, in the person of the head honcho McPherson, has a lot of catching up to do. If he'd wanted to avoid people like me doing what I was at that very moment doing, he should have used a plain envelope. (Mark 2000)

Once again, the author has written a sentence of about 40 words. This one has some of the explanatory quality of the first long sentence, but also represents the mindset and psychology of the protagonist. Readers are now clearer about some of the dramatis personae: it would seem that the 'I' is a sharp, intelligent school pupil who is 'intercepting' a letter from school addressed to the mother. The long sentence is like a rambling monologue, in which the tone is clearly 'anti-school'. We see something of a contempt for the school in the words 'not yet caught up', and the dismissive phrase 'the head honcho', and 'he has a lot of catching up to do'. This same contemptuousness is evident in the third sentence in this paragraph, where the protagonist is suggesting an idea that might have prevented him or her from exercising a 'criminal instinct': 'he should have used'.

The nouns and pronouns are emphasised in interesting ways in this opening of the story. The first paragraph focuses strongly on pronouns – 'I', 'we' and 'mine' – considered above. In the second paragraph the reader is offered more information. We know that one of the concerns of the narrator is that the 'mother' (we are not yet clear that this is the case, but the evidence is growing) has changed her name from Mrs Jagger to Mrs Hague. A wealth of information could be contained in that simple transformation, explained further in the next paragraph. We also know that 'the head honcho' (a phrase we must assume refers to the headteacher) is a Mr McPherson. The reader gains a ready impression that the narrator has little time for his or her school, or those who lead it!

One of the teaching strategies I recommend to accompany this close way of looking at text is to give each pupil a largish envelope containing a number of sheets of A5 plain or lined paper. After reading a line or two lines – or a whole paragraph – each pupil is invited to take out a piece of paper from their envelope, date it and 'put questions to text' which they want the text to reveal, recorded on the paper. Thus, obvious questions to do with the first paragraph would be: 'Who is the "I" of the story?', 'What is contained in the letters?', 'Who are they from?' and so on. Perceptive, experienced readers would be very alert to the change of the woman's surname from Jagger to Hague, and might put a question such as 'Has the narrator's mother recently remarried after a messy divorce?' 'How has the narrator been caused pain?' or 'Is there possibly a problem with a new stepfather?' As the pupils' questions are answered by the gradual revelations in the unfolding narrative, so they put four or five further questions to the text, to which they then await answers as the reading reveals more information.

heathrow nights, by Jan Mark, turns out to be a vivid and realistic story concerning the unhappy Russell, disturbed by his mother's quick remarriage (and, in an open comparison with *Hamlet,* his class visits and ruins a performance of the play!). He is a boy increasingly at odds with his mother, his school and himself. The main part of the story concerns the protagonist and some friends who hide themselves in the anonymity of Heathrow over a half-term period, as Russell begins to work out some insights about himself and his life. Most of the clues about the sort of novel it is and its central concerns are to be found through the type of close reading demonstrated above, employing linguistic knowledge to search a little deeper into meaning.

The same technique may be applied to any text, of course. To illustrate a contrasting story, revealed through similar close scrutiny, I shall consider the opening of Theresa Breslin's *Remembrance:*

Chapter 1

'It's just not quite *respectable.*'

Charlotte took off her cape, hung it on the hallstand and faced her mother's disapproving look. 'It is a Red Cross uniform, Mother, and we are at war. I'm not trying to look respectable. I'm trying to be *useful.*'

Mrs Armstrong-Barnes frowned. 'It is not just the uniform, Charlotte dear. I dare say you think me old-fashioned, but in my opinion it is not quite seemly to bicycle through the village dressed like that. When I was fifteen, young ladies – '

'Mother,' Charlotte interrupted, 'it is a new century and our country is at war. Everyone should help in whatever way they can, and it is quite acceptable now for a young lady to train as a nurse.' Charlotte moved in the direction of the drawing room. 'Has Helen served tea?' (Breslin 2002)

The heading 'Chapter 1' at the top of the page is straightforward, although it is written in a beautiful script-type font, giving some sense of its 'old-world' setting.

The first sentence of this text, while seeming very simple, is actually extremely complex. The book begins in the middle of a conversation that we can easily imagine. The first word of the novel – a contraction, 'It's' – has been chosen deliberately. 'It' is a pronoun, standing in for something already stated. In this instance 'it' represents a whole way of life. The 'it' of this first sentence covers some event or eventuality that has drawn the disapproval of the speaker. The speaker, however, uses three descriptive words – 'just', 'quite' and 'respectable' – that suggest so many nuances and clues about a whole level of society. The verb 'is' (from 'to be') is negatively expressed – 'It's . . . not' – so whatever the 'it' represents it is seen as the reverse of what it should be. But 'it' is not straightforwardly unrespectable, 'it' is 'just not quite' respectable. We are listening to a speaker who is wrapping up the disapproval being expressed in the least demonstrative, careful way by using the modifying adverbs of degree: 'just' and 'quite'. 'Respectable' itself is a significant word. The speaker is expressing a whole set of social mores in choosing that particular adjective and declaring a clear position relative to available behaviours. To give it even more power in this context, the author has chosen to have it printed in italics, thus rendering it even more dramatic by suggesting the manner in which it is to be expressed. Most pupils, apart from the very able, will not discover all those meanings in that one sentence without considerable support, but they should be encouraged to search as carefully as they can, and to be supported in articulating what they discover. Of course, the more practice they have had with such exercises, and the more confident they feel in employing their growing grammar knowledge, the easier those probes will be – and the greater the degrees of revelation.

The second character, Charlotte, who is being addressed by her mother, is not cowed by her words, however. She 'faced' (verb – activity) her mother's 'disapproving' (adjective, offering a better sense of the noun 'look'), clearly as a small act of defiance, and 'faced' also suggests an open look, a 'facing' up to. Thus after only two sentences, the reader is already alert to an intergenerational tension, which will be pursued throughout the novel. The daughter, having hung up her Red Cross cape (such an insignificant uniform to cause unnecessary fuss about, to a modern audience), then turns her mother's words back on her. She repeats the adjective 'respectable' (and the repetition gives it an ironic flavour), but in a couple of sentences with deliberately strong rhetorical power, brings out the patterning of the words.

'I'm not trying to look respectable.
I'm trying to be *useful*.'

This partial repetition is achieved by beginning each sentence with the contraction 'I'm' (I am) that contains part of the verb chain 'am trying to look'/'am trying to be' (where the auxiliary 'be' is followed by the infinitives 'to look' and 'to be' in a very natural English usage), completed by contrasting adjectives 'respectable' and 'useful'. 'Useful' is also printed in italics, to demonstrate that the speaker is referring back to the previous statement and commenting on it with real passion.

'Mrs Armstrong-Barnes frowned.' The double-barrelled name is often a signifier of a higher social class, and so it will be seen in this book. The verb 'frowned' should also be noted. In the last sentence we saw Charlotte 'face' her mother – now we see the mother 'frown'. The author is helping the reader to focus on the facial expressions, and hence – through this close-up – the intimate feelings of the two characters in this scene.

The mother then sets off on a complaint, structured in a characteristic manner. She uses her daughter's name in a way that shows affection on the one hand, but places her in a disapproving position on the other. 'It is not just the uniform, Charlotte dear.' Once again she starts a sentence with 'It', indicating the continuation of the problem she has been presenting since the start of the text. As it is not 'just' (an adverb also meaning 'only' in this instance) the uniform, we realise that she has a whole host of complaints to include in the overall package of 'it'. 'Dear', placed as it is after Charlotte's name, is hugely evocative. It is patronising while still attempting to demonstrate affection. It is also an unusual place to find an adjective, but utterly characteristic of the discourse in the social class already established. The reader should also be alert to certain anachronistic constructions and examples of vocabulary: 'I dare say you think me. . .', 'quite seemly' and 'young ladies' would suggest to the sensitive reader that this story is set many years ago. Indeed, Charlotte has already emphasised the period – 'we are at war', but the mother's words point to a war further back than the 1940s.

Charlotte partly confirms the timing of the narrative by reminding her mother that it is 'a new century' and repeating that 'our country is at war'. She moves the discussion on to another level by suggesting that it is now 'quite acceptable' (note the 'quite' used to modify and draw back the total implications of 'acceptable' used by daughter as well as mother – all suggestive of a restrained dispute, not a furious argument) for 'young ladies' to 'train as nurses'. The shift from the adjective 'respectable' to another, 'acceptable', is an important one. With the intention of changing the focus of their talk she 'moved' to the drawing room (another instance of archaic language), and expresses a wonderful irony of which she is wholly unaware. 'Has Helen served tea?' she asks, without realising that she is still ready to accept that the servants 'serve' and see to the needs of even the most radical of her class! Here we have been presented with a situation in which the traditional behaviours of a certain social class are under threat in the circumstances of war, and in which the younger members circumstances of that society are challenging its conventions – but only up to a point!

Theresa Breslin has written a superb evocation of the First World War, seen from the shared perspectives of two pairs of brothers and sisters, from different social classes, who are drawn more deeply and intensively together and into the harrowing events of that period, often with the disapproval of both sets of parents. Teachers who work carefully with their pupils, examining the text in the way that has been illustrated above, will enable those young people to establish very quickly the major themes of the work. Through this methodology, those pupils should, in turn, be far more prepared to engage with texts unknown to them and discover significant meanings at a far earlier point of the engagement than they might have been used to. Moving on through longer texts in the manner explored above will enable the reader to look more attentively at the meanings being made, and draw more far-reaching conclusions about the wider nature of the work.

The openings of a huge number of texts can be dealt with in the way described above. There is not space here for further detailed study, but one or two superficial studies will suffice. One text familiar to many teachers in Key Stage 3 is Robert Swindells' *Stone Cold*. Two very different characters, a homeless down-and-out and an obsessive former soldier, are set on a dramatic collision course. Their separate first-person narratives tell us a certain amount about each of them, entirely in the language which each employs. The first narrator begins:

You can call me Link. It's not my name, but it's what I say when anybody asks, which isn't often. I'm invisible see? One of the invisible people. Right now I'm sitting in a doorway watching the passers-by. They avoid looking at me. They're afraid I want something they've got, and they're right. They don't want reminding I exist.

The other opens with:

Daily Routine Orders 1

Shelter. Yes. I like it. It's got a ring to it as I'm sure you'll agree. Shelter, as in shelter from the stormy blast. It's what they're all seeking. The street people. What they crave. If they can only find shelter everything will be fine. Well – get fell in, my lucky lads. I'm ready for you.

The first narrator is hesitant, unsure, strongly negative in the statements being made. The name being offered, 'Link', is not a name. A link is, ironically, something which binds, but here it is a tenuous fixing device. The narrator informs the reader 'it's not' his name; but he 'isn't' asked for it often; the passers-by 'don't want' to be reminded of his presence. He is seeking something they have, but do not want to give him. There is an atmosphere of 'fear'. Everything he reflects on makes him worthless or beyond the pale. The second narrator is confident, sharp and certain. The clipped sentences remind us of parade ground imperative discourses ('Well – get fell in, my lucky lads'). He mingles the military with the religious: 'shelter from the stormy blast', reminding the knowledgeable reader of the line from the hymn. There is the device of attempting to woo the audience to his argument: 'as I'm sure you'll agree'. Finally there is the sense of a fully formed plan ready to go into action: 'I'm ready for you.' There could hardly be two further contrasting characters, who must inevitably clash in some way as the novel proceeds.

The issues that have been explored in investigating these openings of fictional narratives have not been the only possible questions that could have been raised, but they have offered sufficient details of a way of working readily available to all teachers of English. An advanced knowledge of grammar is not essential, although a sensitivity to the functions and uses of words, phrases and clauses is necessary.

In the section about 'Grammar knowledge to improve writing', in Chapter 6, I will attempt to show how important it is that these sorts of exercises are not used merely to aid the reading process. They have much greater potential than that, and, as George Keith insists in his chapter 'Noticing grammar':

> The grammatical features are an important part of the relationship between writers and readers created by the discourse of the text. Teaching grammar can be linked to teaching imagination. (Keith 1999)

Comparing the beginnings and endings of texts

Before concluding this chapter, reference should be made to exploring a slightly different approach to texts utilising the same methods. The examples in the previous section have been concerned with looking closely at the beginning of a text or extracts from the text at different points of its development. It is possible to study the beginning of a long text, such as a novel, and then to compare it with the ending. Sometimes, the ending of the text will be a direct reflection of the way in which it began. On other occasions, however, the reader will discover that the narrative has evolved. The end of the narrative now draws on a different register or use of language to bring the story to its resolution. An example of this sort of change through the course of the novel may be found in the increasingly popular modern fantasy *Skellig*, by David Almond (1998).

The first two pages of the novel are dull, bleak and dark. It is a story set at the end of winter. Most images are negative: 'lying there in the darkness behind the tea chests, in the dust and dirt', 'more like a demolition site or rubbish dump', 'shone his little torch into the gloom', 'He'd been dead nearly a week before they found him', and so on. The first-person narrator is depicted as being alone and isolated: 'I found him', 'Nobody else was there. Just me. The others were in the house', 'I didn't want anything to do with him', 'I wanted to get out, to get back to our old house again'. The proper nouns are very interesting at the start of the story – 'Falconer Road', 'Doctor Death' and 'Mr Stone' the estate agent! There is a character, not long born, called 'the baby'.

The final paragraph offers a different perspective. It begins:

She came home on a Sunday. A beautiful bright warm day. It was really spring at last. (Almond 1998)

The 'baby', who has been in hospital, desperately ill for the duration of the novel, is brought home at last.

I lifted the baby higher. She arched her back as if she was about to dance or fly. She reached out, and scratched with her tiny nails at the skin of my face. She tugged at my lips and touched my tongue. She tasted of milk and salt and of something mysterious, sweet and sour all at once. She whimpered and gurgled. I held her closer and her dark eyes looked right into me, right into the place where all my dreams were and she smiled.
(Almond 1998)

The verbs (all those active processes – 'lifted', 'arched', 'to dance', 'fly', 'reached', 'scratched', 'tugged', 'touched', 'tasted', 'whimpered', 'gurgled') in this passage make it crystal clear that the baby is alive and thriving. The baby's increased sensate awareness is conveyed through the contrasting nouns 'milk' and 'salt', then confirmed in the similarly contrasting adjectives 'sweet and sour'. All the worry and fear attached to her earlier in the book, when she was still and powerless, has now been overcome: but the author does not actually tell us that information outright. We find it expressed without equivocation in the language.

The family, so divided and apart at the beginning of the book, is now reunited. The baby is home and they 'didn't know what to say', but 'We just sat there looking at each other and touching each other'. The repetition of 'each other' works powerfully in those phrases to offer an understanding of their togetherness. 'Skellig', so mysterious and unknown in the first pages of the book, has now become a clear picture, 'with his wings rising from his back and a tender smile on his white face'. The gentle and soft images of the angel replace the 'filthy and pale and dried out' impressions from the earlier passage. This novel, which began with the proper noun 'Doctor Death' at the end of its first paragraph, concludes its final paragraph with the new name of the baby: 'Joy'. The transformation is complete.

Teachers might ask their classes to use these close scrutinies of many other novels. *heathrow nights*, for instance, already considered for its opening, ends in the following manner:

'She says I'm drunk,' he said, putting the phone away.
   'You are.'
   'So are you.'
   'I said we were coming right away. I think we'd better.'
   He put on his coat. I picked up the bag.
   'I'll give you a hand with that,' he said, and carefully we wove our way across the crappy pub carpeting to the top of the stairs, toting the bag between us like a carry-cot and clinging to it for dear life, so when we fell down the stairs with it, we were still together at the bottom.

The young narrator has become united with his stepfather, who has arrived at the airport to look for him. At this stage of the novel the lad is now involved in a conspiracy with this man, rather than those friends with whom he was linked at the beginning. They have formed a common bond, finding strength together to resist the displeasure of the mother/wife. Once again we read lots of examples of 'I' and 'we', but presented in a different context from those at the beginning of the book. This time the word 'together' is almost the last word of the novel, and has been preceded in the rather long, rambling sentence (reflecting their drunken, rambling behaviour and speech) by clauses such as 'I'll give you a hand with that', 'toting the bag between us', 'clinging to it', 'we were still together'. They all suggest a partnership simply not present at the start.

Considering closely how authors resolve novels can be a very fruitful way of studying literature. Pupils on the look-out for a potential contrast in the use of language in the beginnings and endings of novels have more interesting ways of getting closer to what they read, and the potential to draw together threads that are sometimes otherwise disregarded. Try this same exercise with Berlie Doherty's *Dear Nobody*, Janni Howker's *Martin Farrell*, Linda Newbery's very fine study of teen fear, *The Damage Done*, and Benjamin Zephaniah's disturbingly real study of human hurt and identity in *face*. Debra Myhill recommends a similar approach with a passage from J. B. Priestley's *An Inspector Calls.* In the Inspector's long speech towards the end of the play beginning, 'But just remember this. . .', readers can trace the way the passage moves from word to clause to sentence level, with the development in the pronouns from 'we' to 'I', as a process of deliberately shifting the sense of responsibility with which the play is concerned.

Non-fiction texts considered closely

All texts may be scrutinised using the same methods. Persuasive texts lend themselves particularly effectively to such an approach, and some are very blatant. Pupils should be encouraged to bring in junk mail from home, and to collect pamphlets about places such as resorts, theme parks and other centres of entertainment. Some are excellent 'starter' texts, extremely useful for encouraging even the least able language users to find examples of grammar they will recognise and be able to comment on. The pamphlet I have in front of me, of a minor stately home, is a good instance. It begins:

—, where Shakespeare's Avon flows gently through the Park, has been the home of the — family, ancestors of the present owner Lady —, since 1430.

Most pupils would have little trouble identifying the types of words performing very specific functions in a richly structured sentence such as this. It is designed to appeal to those seeking heritage, quiet and a sense of the past locked still in the present. 'Shakespeare's' is used adjectivally, and regularly overused in that manner. For all who visit Warwickshire, every county boundary sign informs incomers that they are now entering 'Shakespeare's' county! The 'Avon' does not merely 'flow', but does so 'gently'. There are not just grounds attached to this house, but a 'Park' – and the capital letter is there in the original.

The rooms come in for the same treatment, very much in keeping with the cover, for example:

The Ballroom, grandly resplendent in pink and gold, has a fine coved ceiling with four trompe l'oeil shell corners.

The mellow panelled Library is lined with over five thousand books, as well as many interesting manuscripts, the oldest dating from 1150.

The peaceful Drawing rooms, with their lovely portraits and elegant furniture, overlook the Park.

Almost every noun is embellished with an adjective – 'resplendent', 'fine', 'mellow panelled', 'interesting', 'peaceful', 'lovely', 'elegant'. Collect these words together, removed from the nouns they enhance, and it is possible to reconstruct the whole atmosphere being 'sold' through the leaflet: quiet, rich, tasteful refinement! There is much technical vocabulary too: 'coved ceiling', 'trompe l'oeil shell corners', likely to turn on the knowledgeable, and prove to be a hook for the uninitiated!

When my children were much younger it used to be a family game to look for such words in restaurants and other food outlets. Menus are a rich source of adjectives and noun phrases, in the process of making their goods sound more appetising. Pupils should be encouraged to collect menus, leaflets and other printed material offering a 'hard sell' of culinary products. My English adviser colleague in Bedfordshire, Simon Wrigley, contrasts two eating establishment menus, and invites pupils to inform him for which social class of diner they think each was devised. One has such dishes as:

'Toad in the Hole' (tasty pork sausages, baked in batter and served with mashed potato, a selection of vegetables and onion gravy)
and 'Lasagne Verde' (a traditional Italian recipe. Layers of pasta, with lean minced beef in a rich Bolognese sauce. Served with garlic bread).

The other has:

'Rack of Lamb Provence' (baked in the oven with a Savoury Herb Crust [sic] with a Rosemary Jus) and 'Scampi Tail Frits Andalouse' (Deep fried and served with a Tomato and Pepper Mayonnaise), served with Courgette Frits, Minted garden Peas, Rissoles and Boulange Potatoes.

The particular mixture of nouns, adjectives and verbs is very evocative, and wholly in tune with the aspirations and likely customer appeal in each establishment. There is obvious study to be made of the tone and 'voice' of each menu, as well as names of dishes. What is so noticeable in the second menu is the liberal sprinkling of capital letters to words that are not strictly proper nouns. Pupils will be interested to speculate why the managers of the establishment have produced their printed materials with such liberties of punctuation!

A Scottish company offers ready-cooked meals by post, and sells them in the following manner:

Tart of Red Onion & Camembert

No wonder this tasty tart is so popular with Scottish Gourmet customers! They've discovered the delicious combination of caramelised onions and Camembert cheese, bound together in a light and herby egg cream and baked in a pastry case. A superbly savoury vegetarian treat.

Healthy Cranachan

Toasted rolled oats and chopped dates stirred into a smooth blend of cheese, natural yoghurt, clear honey and lemon juice. A wee dram of whisky adds a restorative glow to this low fat dessert, part of an imaginative range of recipes specially devised for those who are watching what they eat.

Christmas Game Pie

Whisky and brandy enrich the gravy in this luscious meaty pie filled with goose, pheasant, pigeon, hare, rabbit, Red Deer venison and Aberdeen Angus beef, quickly sealed in hot butter and simmered until tender with root vegetables and herbs. Tip into a pie dish to reheat, sealing in the flavours with the puff pastry lid provided. Just one of the festive favourites featured each December in Scottish Gourmet's comprehensive Christmas menu.

Just as pupils were recommended to isolate the adjectives from the nouns they modified in the leaflet about the English country house in the example given above, so they might try the same activity with those related to food, to see what sort of collection they achieve. From the examples given above they would derive, among others: 'tasty', 'delicious', 'savoury', 'light', 'smooth', 'natural', 'clear', 'luscious', and 'hot'. (Actually, each one of these three texts, although related, differs slightly from the others, and able pupils would distinguish those differences by close linguistic investigation.) There is frequent use of alliteration in these pieces: 'tasty tart', 'superbly savoury', 'festive favourites featured' and 'comprehensive Christmas'. Alliteration is much better explored in contexts such as this, where pupils might suggest why the copywriter has been so self-indulgent with its use.

Just as relevant in these pieces is the study of the use of verbs. Words such as 'enrich', 'filled', 'sealed', 'bound' and 'stirred' give a sense of personal attention and quality to satisfy the particularly developed tastes of the customer.

A furniture retail outlet recently printed an advertising supplement to be distributed inside magazines, entitled 'Brand spanking new sexy sofas' ('Geddit?' as Glenda Slagg in *Private Eye* might say). Its copy reads as follows:

> Pick up the sofa of your dreams with our brand spanking new collection of sexy – sofas.
>
> Our unique mix of passion and fashion will make you go weak at the knees! And whichever you fancy – they're all within easy reach – with seductively low introductory prices, 4 years free credit and everything free for a year.
>
> So get ready for this tantalising glimpse of the sexiest sofas around.

And later:

> Be adventurous with a fiery sexy sofa from —. Designed to get your pulse racing, in colours that will stir your emotions and set the mood for love.
>
> So whatever your taste we'll have something exciting and daring for you at an equally exciting price. That's the joy of —.

'Nuff said', as another popular expression goes. A few enterprising pupils will be able to use such models for their own purposes.

A sandwich pack I was sold is another rich text source. This is the message printed on one side:

> This —**Box** isn't just a box, it's a guarantee that the **sandwich** inside has been made here and now in your local —. Because our —**Box** is cardboard and not plastic it cannot be heat-sealed or gas flushed. It won't hold long-life factory sandwiches commonly available these days. The —**Box** goes soggy. Just like a good sandwich, it has a very short life. No preservatives, no distribution depots, no 'sell by' dates and definitely no nappy pads. At the end of **each day** we would rather give away all our unsold sandwiches than compromise **our standards**.

Pupils will not only want to think about the language being employed in a piece such as this, bearing in mind its commercial context, but will also speculate as to why certain words have been highlighted in the manner illustrated.

Such texts are the stuff of everyday civilisation. We encounter them in virtually every walk of life. The tables in the atrium canteen area in the office where I work are used for meetings most of the day, although they should be available for catering purposes at lunchtime. However, many people were allowing their meetings to continue into lunchtime. This notice was then placed on all tables:

> If you are having a meeting please note these tables must be vacated between 11.45am and 2.00pm for the lunch service.
> Thank you for your co-operation.

We might regard such a text as unremarkable. Many English teachers might think that it certainly does not warrant close classroom study; we have our time taken up with far more important texts. But I think it does deserve attention. It is written by canteen staff who are not used to writing formal notices. It has some interesting moments of awkwardness, such as 'If you are having a meeting'; most writers accustomed to writing such messages would employ the verb 'hold'. There is no 'lunch service'; the writer means for the use of 'those eating/purchasing lunch'. Such notices are frequently to be found in community centres and other spaces where people meet. Close study of them often shows an overlapping of different writing cultures. The writer wants to be authoritarian, but not overly so. Therefore 'must be vacated' is contrasted with the 'thank you for your co-operation'. There is a distinct social uncertainty about the text:

> the unsureness about how to represent the relations between the writers and the readers, in their social roles. Should these be clear and unambiguous rules, authoritative, perhaps authoritarian, or should they be relatively friendly demands or statements? . . . This approach to text gives a student insight into the reasons for the existence of generic forms of text, and at the same time equips her or him with knowledge, principles and skills on the basis of which they can understand their own text-making, and shape that successfully to their ends. (Kress 1995)

I agree with Gunter Kress when he writes:

> Mundane texts are overlooked; yet they are the texts which are most telling, in many ways, in our everyday and working lives. They form the bedrock of social and economic life. Without an understanding of the mundane text, and without the confident ability to use it for one's purposes in whatever domain, we cannot be fully effective participants in the economic, social and political life of our group. Moreover, without a deep understanding of the mundane text we are cut off from the full appreciation of the aesthetically valued text. (*ibid.*)

There is an important place for these texts in English study, and they should be encouraged. Collecting such examples will continue to inspire pupils to take more notice of the way language is used around them, which often shapes their experiences. Teachers might challenge a class to find a wide range of different examples.

Magazines are a rich source for textual study. Collections of magazines are readily available, and teachers could soon gather together a large variety. Pupils could be asked to pay close regard to the language of different examples, possibly to ascertain the intended audience. The questions they might ask could be:

- What are the linguistic characteristics of *Sugar* that make it so distinctly focused on young women?
- How different is the language of *FHM* or *Loaded*?
- What differences in language can be distinguished between women's magazines, such as *Woman and Home* and *Cosmopolitan*?
- Teachers might try to find examples of women's magazines from 30 or 40 years ago – or even longer. How has the language changed in the meantime? The advertisements are especially interesting.

The following piece is a favourite of mine, taken from *Good Housekeeping*:

> This is the time of year to espouse the escapist school of cookery. Fine weather should encourage you to throw open the doors and spend time with the children, friends, the garden. Build meals around precious summer rituals and leave time for visiting a romantic garden, picking fruit with a chum, or swimming in the river.
>
> Slow food that simmers in the bottom of the stove or marinates in the fridge comes into its own now. As do instant meals made up from a few eggs, and salads and herbs from the garden. Or what about a bit of backyard bartering, where you swap your glut of blackcurrants for your neighbour's plum tart? (*Good Housekeeping*, July 1998)

Once again, the adjectives offer an easy starting point – 'escapist', 'fine', 'precious', 'romantic'. But the nouns are also very interesting: 'school of cookery', 'rituals', 'chum', 'bartering' and 'glut'. Note the use of the idea of 'time', as in 'now is the time', and 'leave time', and the 'slow meals' and 'instant meals'. The last sentence of the extract cuts across the dreamy, sun-bathed reverie of the preceding statements to ask a question. What is the author intending by this device? How does this lifestyle equate with that of your pupils? I cannot resist another short burst from the same article:

> Splash out with your brightest china, your favourite plates, generous

glasses and big napkins. Finding just the right turquoise pot to serve thick yoghurt in makes a difference. If you go to the seaside for picnics, it's worth taking big, handsome ceramic bowls to serve food in, even if it is a hard walk across the sand. And if you spot samphire growing behind the dunes, it can be picked, washed and tossed in a salad for its salty taste. Keep the mood robust and colourful with a tablecloth made from a lovely old shawl, plump cushions, a basket to hold plates, and cutlery wrapped in oversized cotton squares that will do well for wiping sticky fingers. (*ibid.*)

Other magazines have their own, very distinguishable features, and pupils of all ages and abilities in secondary school can be given some appropriate material on which to make their own comments. The following, from the *Radio Times*, comes very close to spoken language, and makes all sorts of commentary on the programme being advertised:

Drama
Casualty
8.15 p.m. BBC1

Casualty returns tonight, for its 17th series, with one of those blood-and-guts stories that are always the consequence of introducing a particularly cumbersome piece of machinery into this perennially successful hospital soap.

Tonight, no-nonsense consultant Harry (Simon MacCorkindale) takes his family of selfish and not particularly pleasant children on a day out at Holby county fair. But a sky-diving display goes badly wrong, necessitating Harry calling in the air ambulance. And wouldn't you just know it – the ambulance crashes after take-off, leaving the field littered with the most appalling carnage.

Now, if you look closely at this crash, it might be hard to see how on earth all these people came to be so badly hurt, or even dead. But there you have it, sophisticated machinery always causes havoc in *Casualty*.

Harry is thus forced to take command of a dreadful situation, and has to carry out some particularly tricky on-site surgery within the stricken helicopter. But that's the great thing about Harry, a much needed figure of authority in *Casualty*. (*Radio Times*, 14–20 September 2002)

Pupils will quickly be able to distinguish the plot from the commentary. They are likely to notice the phrases usually associated with speech – 'wouldn't you just know it', 'Now, if you look', 'But there you have it', 'But that's the great thing'. The word 'particularly' appears three times in the extract and there is a liberal use of hyphenated words. These characteristics are typical of the language seen regularly in tabloid newspapers.

Newspapers can also be studied with a strong focus on language. At least three types of writing are evident for pupils to recognise: tabloid, semi-tabloid and broadsheet. Comparing stories about the same topic from the *Sun,* the *Daily Mail* and the *Independent,* for instance, will enable pupils to establish three sorts of style at work in the press. Pupils should concentrate on vocabulary, sentence length, and the aspects of construction that enable the newspaper to 'frame' their stories in certain ways. Newspaper reports and stories are rarely neutral; they usually have a point of view to express. Employing the passive voice is a device very common in journalism and is a powerful way of making the reader shift attention from the perpetrator to the victim. Thus, a newspaper sympathetic to the police would not report:

Police beat protesters,

but might go so far as to share the same information in the following manner, if somewhat evasively:

Protesters beaten by police.

Pupils of all abilities should be given guided direct contact with newspapers, to begin identifying some of the linguistic tricks and games they play. At the very least, pupils could be afforded some insight into the appalling punning so characteristic of the *Sun.* More able pupils will discover important contrasts in comparing the 'leaders' of different newspapers, particularly in pinning down the sorts of persuasive language used in each.

Using grammar to make meaning in poetry

Far too many young people dislike or know too little about poetry. The study of *Children's Reading Choices* undertaken by Christine Hall and Martin Coles, published in 1999, questioning the personal reading interests of 8000 pupils between 10 and 14 years old, revealed that very few chose to read poetry during the period of the survey. The statistics relating to this research could probably be verified by most children's librarians and booksellers. Most adolescents only really encounter poetry in school.

English teachers want their pupils to enjoy poetry, and to feel sufficiently empowered to find their way through it independently, to recognise how powerfully language is at work, and how poetry has the means to offer so much more than its literal, initial meanings to the discerning reader. Yet, oddly, the linguistically analytical approach is not one that has been employed very often in helping pupils to engage more closely with poetry; teachers have tended to encourage personal response in an evaluative rather than a descriptive manner. Barbara Bleiman, in an article about integrating language and literature approaches to A level texts (but from which a similarly integrated approach may be seen as beneficially possible for pupils in Key Stages 3 and 4), suggested:

> And what's more, it suddenly becomes clear how much more there is to say about *literary* texts when language issues are examined in more detail. Of course literature students have always been asked to talk about language. No student writing about literature could hope to get a high grade, from KS 3 through to A level, without writing about language. It's just that they're expected to do it using only their eyesight, when they could be offered a really good high definition microscope. (Bleiman 1999)

Boys in particular enjoy and positively respond to having more substantial, concrete issues on which to build any textual exploration or analysis. As boys read less poetry (Hall and Coles 1999) and achieve standards between 10 and 15 per cent worse than girls in tests at the end of Key Stages 3 and 4, an approach to poetry using more explicit linguistic knowledge could be an effective way of helping boys to close that attainment gap – and improve their enjoyment of the subject.

Part of the problem I was able to identify from my own teaching experiences had to do with how little pupils know to enable them to find accessible ways into the poem, particularly those examples that seemed to present initial difficulties. Some of the following suggestions are ways of enabling pupils to form a more immediate relationship with a poem, to establish a sort of 'intellectual foothold' from which further forays into the overall meaning may be launched. Of course, the approach articulated earlier in this chapter (see pages 96–8) about generic questions to raise concerning any text apply equally firmly to more positive encounters with poetry just as much as any other sort of work.

Pupils should try to establish immediately who is '*speaking*' the words of the poem. Seeking the pronouns is a helpful starting device. Many poems are in the first person (occasionally in the plural – 'we'), some are addressed to the reader in the second person, and a few are about third-person participants. Quite often the voice might be unrecognisable, a detached point of view relating an event, or informing the reader about somebody or something, but even that understanding contributes to the meaning. As an early tactic of engagement, encourage pupil readers to establish the identification of who is carrying out the address, or to whom it is being made. One important word of warning is necessary here: inexperienced pupils, or those who know little of poetry, often have trouble disentangling the 'voice' of the poem from the poet! They have to be helped to see that a point of view is being expressed, but not necessarily that of the poet.

To practise this tactic in a very straightforward exercise, teachers could select any worthwhile anthology of poetry and work through the first few lines of each poem until the majority of pupils in the class are able to identify the pronouns that indicate who is the 'speaker', or who or what is being 'spoken to'. Many will be extremely simple:

> '*I* had a little brother
> And *I* brought him to *my* mother. . .' (Mary Ann Hoberman)

> '*My* heart is like a singing bird,
> Whose nest is in a watered shoot. . .' (Christina Rossetti)

Some poems will take longer to reveal these matters. Elizabeth Jennings, in her poem 'One Flesh', has already written two and a half stanzas of six lines each, before stating:

> Do they know they're old,
> These two who are *my* father and mother
> Whose fire, from which *I* came, has now grown cold.

In some examples, the 'I' and 'we' might well need further questioning to move closer to the central meaning, as in Edwin Muir's 'The Horses':

> Barely a twelvemonth after
> The seven days war that put the world to sleep,
> Late in the evening the horses came.
> By then *we* had made our covenant with silence,
> But in the first few days it was so still
> *We* listened to our breathing and were afraid.

Other questions, based on a language focus, may also be put to poems, to enable pupils to reveal areas of meaning. What sort of sentence, for instance, is used at the start of a poem?

- A *statement* (most usual)?
  I sit in the top of the wood, my eyes closed.
  Inaction, no falsifying dream
  Between my hooked head and hooked feet:
  Or in sleep rehearse perfect kills and eat.
  ('Hawk Roosting' by Ted Hughes)

- A *question* (quite often)?
  O what is that sound which so thrills the ear
    Down in the valley drumming, drumming?
  Only the scarlet soldiers, dear,
    The soldiers coming. ('O What is that Sound?' by W. H. Auden)

- A *command* (sometimes)?
  Do not go gentle into that good night,
  Old age should burn and rave at close of day;
  Rage, rage against the dying of the light.
    ('Do not go gentle into that Good Night' by Dylan Thomas)

- Or an *exclamation* (infrequent)?
      How beautiful is the rain!
      After the dust and heat,
      In the broad and fiery street
      In the narrow lane,
      How beautiful is the rain!
      How it clatters along the roofs,
      Like the tramp of hoofs!
      ('Rain in Summer' by Henry Wadsworth Longfellow)

Other 'establishing' questions pupils could be encouraged to put include:

- How many poems complete a sentence in the first two lines, and how many take much longer to develop fully?
- Where is the first main verb of the poem?
- Which poems are built on 'naturalistic' language, like the normal language of pupils' writing, and which are contracted or condensed for particular effect?
- How many poems use no punctuation at all, and yet still seem to make sense?
- Is there an obvious relationship between the poem's title and the first two lines of the poem?
- How many poems begin with subordinate clauses, signalled by words such as 'although', 'however' or 'perhaps'?

These exercises will enable pupils to make some interesting discoveries about the ways poems open, how they employ different 'voices', and how to begin to engage with a poem from first contact. They will also help readers to prepare for more complex issues of analysis when they are older, and dealing with more challenging poetry. Thomas Hardy's poem 'The Oxen' is an example of a poem where the 'speaker – I' is attempting to contrast two periods, a 'then' and a now, 'in these years'. Knowing that there is one speaker is not enough; the language has to be scoured much more closely to capture this detail.

The Oxen

Christmas Eve, and twelve of the clock,
'Now they are all on their knees',
An elder said as we sat in a flock
By the embers in hearthside ease.

We pictured the meek mild creatures where
They dwelt in their strawy pen,
Nor did it occur to one of us there
To doubt they were kneeling then.

So fair a fancy few would weave
In these years! Yet, I feel
If someone said on Christmas Eve,
'Come; see the oxen kneel

In the lonely barton by yonder coomb
Our childhood used to know.'
I should go with him in the gloom,
Hoping it might be so.

In seeking ways in which pronouns are used in this poem, the reader will notice how the 'we' and 'us' of the first half becomes 'I' in the second half. There is a clear suggestion that some collaborative, shared sense of a speaker at work in the first eight lines has shifted to a more personal, perhaps exposed perspective in the second half.

Applying a broader linguistic analysis to this poem helps to illustrate how vividly and comprehensively the past is contrasted with the present. The first two stanzas, representing the past, are relatively simply constructed; yet the present, written about in the final two stanzas, is dealt with in a more complex manner. The sentences of the first eight lines are mostly patterned in a main clause followed by a subordinate clause structure. The 'sentence blocks' also fit the line shape, no 'block of meaning' going on beyond two lines. However, the final eight lines break up that neat shaping, the main 'block of meaning' in this section starting in line 11 and continuing to the end of line 15. A close consideration of the poem's tenses indicates that the prevailing tense in the first half is of the past ('said', 'sat', 'pictured', 'dwelt', 'were kneeling'); while the second half is predominantly in the present tense ('would weave', 'feel', 'come; see', 'hoping'). The use of modal verbs also confirms the vital realisation of the split in the poem, so necessary for understanding its meanings. There are no modal verbs in the first half of the poem, while 'would', 'should' and 'might' modify ideas in the second part. Readers may reasonably surmise that the certainties of the first part, set perhaps in the more innocent times of childhood when the nativity story is more readily accepted, have become less sure in later life, when adult scepticism has developed.

One other example of detailed grammatical analysis will serve to demonstrate how pupils can be helped to find some effective ways of discovering meaning in poems by applying some straightforward linguistic questions.

Ozymandias

I met a traveller from an antique land
Who said: Two vast and trunkless legs of stone
Stand in the desert. Near them, on the sand,
Half sunk, a shattered visage lies, whose frown
And wrinkled lip, and sneer of cold command
Tell that its sculptor well these passions read
Which yet survive (stamped on these lifeless things)
The hand that mocked them and the heart that fed:
And on the pedestal these words appear:
'My name is Ozymandias, King of Kings:
Look on my works, ye Mighty, and despair!'
Nothing beside remains. Round the decay
Of that colossal wreck, boundless and bare
The lone and level sands stretch far away.
(Percy Bysshe Shelley)

There are a number of activities which pupils can undertake with a text such as this. It is self-evidently a sonnet, which may serve as a starting point. It is a poem typical of a literary period, and could attract attention within the context of the literary tradition. Poetic devices, such as alliteration and rhyme, are at work in the poem, and might offer another approach. The following exercises are based on its linguistic contents.

How many sentences make up the poem? There are four. What are the lengths of the sentences? The first is 21 words long; the second contains 69 words; the third is three words long! The final sentence comprises 18 words. The contrast of 69 words, directly juxtaposed with a sentence of only three words, suggests that any reader needs to raise questions about such a discrepancy. It is worth considering how condensed those three words are: 'Nothing beside remains'. The first word is a total negative, 'nothing'; and the whole sentence is a concentrated way of expressing how virtually everything has disappeared. What has gone? Well, the previous two lines contain the arrogantly declamatory, all-powerful legend once carved at the base of a huge statue:

> My name is Ozymandias, King of Kings:
> Look on my works, ye Mighty, and despair!

Yet it has nearly all gone. The apparently indestructible, everlasting symbol of one person's rule has been destroyed. Such power is, after all, a myth. But other words and phrases in the poem also confirm that sense of decay and the broken down. Careful exploration will discover the adjectives 'trunkless' and 'lifeless' – the repetition of the suffix 'less' gives a sense of diminishment. This idea is also supported by adjectives and nouns: 'sunk', 'shattered', 'decay' and 'wreck'.

In a number of ways, the linguistically interested reader is able to discover how this poem is concerned with destruction and disintegration, not only of physical artefacts but also of the overblown pomposity of human power. All dictators, from ancient history to Hitler and Saddam Hussein, have continued to believe that their spirit will live forever in their (usually awful) grandiose statues and pictorial representations.

Considering the 'voices' of 'Ozymandias' can also motivate greater interest. The poem begins with the speaker 'I', but then the traveller takes over, telling of the evidence of this destroyed statue in the desert. Yet the statue has a declaration too:

> My name is Ozymandias, King of Kings:
> Look on my works, ye Mighty, and despair!,

bellowing loudly to all those unfortunate enough to encounter his authority.

I really do not believe that this sort of reading of poetry detracts in any way from its enjoyment. Indeed, for some less enthusiastic readers, particularly some groups of able but reluctant boys, this open-ended approach gives them a range of different pathways to discover something of the core of the poems they have to study. They may not make all their judgements based on linguistic considerations alone, but they can become more confident about making evaluations and other literary estimations when searching from a more secure position.

A poet such as Kit Wright, with his delicate and evocative poem 'The Magic Box', reminds us how much beauty and what a full picture can be conveyed without resorting to adjectives all the time, instead relying heavily on nouns:

> I will put in the box
> the swish of a silk sari on a summer night,
> fire from the nostrils of a Chinese dragon,
> the tip of a tongue touching a tooth.
>
> I will put in the box
> a snowman with a rumbling belly
> a sip of the bluest water from Lake Lucerne
> a leaping spark from an electric fish.

Teachers will look out for other excellent examples of this sort of approach if they realise that pupils will achieve success by discovering some of the traits that contribute to the meaning.

Reading the environment

The final activity may be conducted on a number of occasions as pupils progress year on year. Its main aim is for pupils to genuinely notice the language of the environment. They are taken either for a stroll around the school premises or even further afield, into the local environment or immediate neighbourhood of the school.

On these walks they would be expected to take note and record instances of different sorts of texts, and the functions those texts are fulfilling. Are they instructing, informing, persuading, explaining, warning, or doing something else? These texts may be found on notices, formal and informal, house agents' 'for sale/sold' signs, painted on the road or pavement or over a shop window, on the sides of lorries, vans or buses, street furniture, mechanical implements, rubbish bins, garden gates or street signs.

Pupils should be encouraged to pay particular attention to shop signs they might not notice normally. Many shops have characteristic signs, such as hairdressers. They are often called 'The Top Knot', or 'A Cut Above', or 'The Short and Curlies'. Pupils may notice much more mundane titles, such as 'The Village Stores', or 'Filkin and Son, Hardware Merchants'. It does not matter, as long as they begin to consider what tasks language is fulfilling. The hairdressers mentioned above are all examples of noun phrases, and pupils might be asked to think about other contexts in which they come across noun phrases. They are, of course, regularly found in titles of texts – more often fiction than non-fiction. Thus on the fiction shelves it is not unusual to come across such titles as *Pride and Prejudice*, *A Kestrel for a Knave*, *A Midsummer Night's Dream*, *Twelfth Night*, *Lord of the Rings*, *The Lion, the Witch and the Wardrobe*. Non-fiction texts have a greater tendency to be in the mould of 'How to. . .', or 'Discovering more about. . .', but not entirely so. This manner of titling would make yet another subject of study for a class.

CHAPTER 6

Using Grammar to Improve Writing

At the heart of good writing are the dual qualities of creating and crafting. Perhaps in the past we have tended to view these as opposites, suggesting that any active 'interference' with a child's writing might stifle creativity. Perhaps at the present time we are tending to over-value grammatical exhibitionism, the urge to demonstrate grammatical knowledge without grammatical understanding. But thinking of creativity and crafting as opposites misses the fundamental point, that to be creative you have to be able to shape, craft and manipulate language for effect. Thinking of them as opposites also leads to unhelpful ideological polarisations: the liberal, left-wing creativity camp versus the conservative right-wing grammar camp. The effective teaching of writing sets writing in a context, values the voice of the child *and* teaches explicitly how he or she can craft language creatively for effect, through looking closely at the linguistic features of texts. (Myhill 2001b)

In the above quotation, Debra Myhill has succeeded in capturing the essential core of recent, sometimes quite fierce arguments about whether pupils can actually improve their writing by bringing an overt knowledge of grammar to it. Like Tony Burgess (quoted on p. 37), however, Myhill has suggested very firmly that a synthesis is the only possible realistic approach to this discussion. This book has been posited on that same view, and will continue to explore the value of assisting pupils to become better writers by focusing on some of the linguistic and structural features of their composition, as well as offering them worthwhile subjects to write about.

Traditionally, the detail of writing has not been taught so readily in English, as may be seen so often in the comments that used to be added to pieces of work marked and assessed by teachers. It was not unusual to see responses such as 'Mind your punctuation', or 'Be careful with sentence construction', or 'Poor paragraphing' – sometimes in the same work – without helpful suggestions that might prevent repetition of the same mistakes in the future. Most teachers offered generalised advice about 'good openings', or 'topic sentences', or 'finishing with a flourish – know how you will conclude before you begin' and so on – yet rarely provided a focus for enhancing control and bringing about planned improvement. Pupils who have been unable to understand 'the point' of writing or cannot see why they need to learn to express themselves in a number of contexts in this way (many of whom are male), have been hugely disadvantaged as a consequence.

Roger Beard (2000) refers to nearly 500 studies of writing reviewed by George Hillocks (1986, 1995) through which he identified four broad teaching approaches which are set out briefly below:

- *Presentational* – often found in English course books, involving teachers imparting knowledge before writing, and resulting in the teacher setting tasks and marking the outcomes;
- *'Natural process' and individualised* – found in the work of Graves (1983) and Calkins (1986), involving engaging pupils in writing and fostering positive dispositions towards writing topics chosen by the pupils, which passed through general procedures, e.g. multiple drafts and peer comments;
- *'Guided writing'* (what Hillocks calls an 'environmental approach') – suggested through the research of Scardamalia (1981) and Martin (1989), involving the teacher inducing and supporting active learning of complex strategies that pupils are not capable of using on their own, resulting in negotiated writing that develops materials and activities to engage pupils in task-specific processes. (Beard 2001)

Hillocks claims that the 'Guided writing' approach was 'two or three times more effective than the natural process/individualised approaches and over four times more effective than the presentational approach' (Hillocks 1995).

Debra Myhill makes a similar sort of analysis when she writes:

in the process approach, writing is used as a tool to develop the writer, giving him or her a voice and allowing inner feelings and thoughts to be given expression and validity. The teacher is an enabler of the child's personal growth and self-awareness, rather than being in any way instrumental in developing the child's writing. Likewise, the genre approach inducts writers into the dominant genres of our culture, inviting writers to imitate and replicate the available genres. The emphasis is on the form of the genre, much less upon its linguistic features, and writers are much more likely to be set the task of writing in a particular genre than to study explicitly the linguistic characteristics of that genre. What . . . both approaches (and the earlier product approach) have in common is that they are stronger on why children are writing than on how to help them become better writers. (Myhill 2001a)

At this point it is necessary to remind readers that there are strong detractors of this position, including Pat D'Arcy (n.d., 2001), Neil Allen (2002), Michael Rosen (2002) and Mary Hilton (2001), whose position has already been considered in more detail in the Introduction. Philip Pullman, the novelist, also made a vituperative attack on the way writing was being 'framed' and encouraged in the National Literacy Strategy in an address, *Perverse, All Monstrous, All Prodigious Things*, to the National Association for the Teaching of English (NATE) Conference (2002). Although I support the application of more specifically focused objectives outlined in the KS 3 *Framework* document, I am greatly disappointed that the NLS was unable to offer a clear model of language learning on which to base the integrative teaching and learning of language.

Establishing that pupils know the structures and simple grammatical features of writing

'Closed exercises', from which pupils extrapolate broader learning

While there should be an increasingly universal expectation by secondary schools that the children arriving in their intake year will have some knowledge of the ways language works in different sorts of text, this knowledge will vary from school to school and pupil to pupil. Secondary English teachers will be interested in discovering exactly what their pupils can recognise, and how they use that knowledge to *control* what takes place in their writing endeavours. Teachers will ultimately want their pupils to enter writing engagements confidently aware of, and able to sustain, their control over the different linguistic opportunities available to them. Making it possible to practise those options is an important preparatory criterion for improved writing success.

All the suggested exercises below should never be conducted in isolation. Ideally, they should follow some exploratory reading, where texts of different sorts would be considered first, the 'purposes' of those texts discussed and pupils then challenged to offer ideas about why the authors of those texts made the linguistic choices they did. There is no suggestion that these approaches to writing are offered in a chronological, progressive manner. Some will be appropriate and relevant for particular pupils, while others would serve different purposes. They all, however, give point to teaching areas of language, and apply the knowledge acquired in such study in practical ways. They are offered merely as examples of the sorts of worthwhile grammatical contexts that can be made available in English classrooms (and, occasionally, those of teachers of other subjects).

An early exercise with a new class might be to ask pupils, either individually, in pairs or in groups (in 'guided writing' contexts), to construct a piece of writing – probably a **recount** (since pupils are used to employing that genre in commonplace instances, such as storytelling, or the relating of autobiographical events) using only a specified number of **simple sentences** (with no other alternative). Even greater attention could be given to the manner in which they are writing by insisting that pupils must compose their sentences in a strict subject–verb (possibly object or adverbial) (**SVOA**) order (having first paid some regard to checking how often particular authors might use that same order). All the **verbs** should be identified actively during the actual writing by being circled, and must be in the past tense. The subject matter or the event to be recounted, of course, is entirely up to the pupils. For example:

- I went to the rec on Saturday. I played football with my friends. My team won. We went home at eight o'clock. I enjoyed myself.

Depending on how able the teacher believes the pupils to be, they may be given very specific instructions about how many sentences to write. In this instance more able pupils would be asked to write more sentences than their less confident peers. Another issue of differentiation could be the amount of text, or what features of the text, pupils are required to mark (underline/colour/circle, etc.) as they are writing.

Assessment could be based on two areas of consideration in such an exercise: how close the performance of writing was to strictly defined criteria, and how well the pupil was able to comment on and discuss the implications of being asked to write in this manner. Most pupils are likely to have something to say about the following:

- how boring such a way of writing is for the writer;
- how uninteresting this way of writing is for the reader;
- how easy it might be to slip into an unthinking routine;
- how difficult it is to include special sorts of effects in this sort of work;
- whether it would be possible to use this formula with any sorts of text.

They should also be asked to articulate any frustrations they experienced through being prevented from writing exactly what they wanted to write.

An exercise of this sort may be applied at any time within the Key Stage 3 curriculum to ensure that pupils are reminding themselves of the issues involved, and improving their ability to consider its implications. This exercise is never an end in itself. It is always worthwhile for the other learning and textual matters it is capable of highlighting.

Learning the differences between simple, compound and complex sentences

Without suggesting in any way that sentence structuring is hierarchical, pupils may be encouraged to vary their **simple sentences** with **compound sentences** and **complex sentences**. Teachers should not feel constrained about stipulating very specifically just what any piece of writing should comprise in this sort of learning context. Thus, in the early stages, it would probably offend the instincts of many teachers to require pupils to write the following:

- a recount passage of one, two or three paragraphs (perhaps depending on ability), each paragraph consisting of:
  – one simple, one compound and one complex sentence;
  – no sentence to be more than 12 words in length;
  – the simple and compound sentences have to follow a **SVO** pattern.
(e.g. *My mum and I took our baby to the hospital. I waited in the entrance and mum and the baby visited the doctor. Luckily, with the right treatment, she should get better soon.*)

Some of these exercises may present considerable difficulties for a few pupils (although weaker boy writers like to employ a tightly structured outline in their writing, particularly when they feel unsure about the task), so teachers might think it more appropriate to 'model' the requirements for them – such as the example offered above.

An example of writing support I have seen working very successfully with much younger pupils, enabling them to pay attention to what they are attempting, explaining what they are doing, yet still allowing them to speak wholly in their own voice, is demonstrated in the following exercise. Once again, there would be an expectation that pupils are already familiar with texts working in this manner.

Pupils are asked to write their 'news' (another way of representing **recount**) to the following criteria:

- a four-sentence paragraph;
- all the sentences to be **statements**;
- the first and last sentences to be **simple sentences**;
- the middle two sentences to be **compound sentences**;

- the first sentence – the orientation – to state who took part, where and when;
- the last sentence – the reorientation – to sum up the event;
- all **verbs** to be in the past tense;
- words or phrases of chronology (the passing of time) should be included. (e.g. *On Saturday my Nan and I shopped in town. We left home after breakfast and went on the bus. Nan bought me a coke and chips at dinnertime and she had a pie and cup of tea. I really enjoyed the day.*)

If pupils in Key Stages 1 and 2 can write in this sort of 'frame' – and they can – teachers should be exploring with older pupils other, more challenging possibilities. Having begun to write in an increasingly assured manner by using these supports, pupils should also be assisted in transforming some parts of their work to meet other demands on them when they are ready.

This approach has a substantial academic pedigree. Roger Beard cites the research of Mina Shaughnessy (1977) in New York:

> Central to Shaughnessy's analysis is a recognition that syntactical difficulties are signs of unfamiliarity with certain features of formal written English. Shaughnessy reminds us that many of these errors are from attempts to manage more academic and impersonal writing. This kind of writing may require the kinds of formal, complex sentences that are rarely used in speech. She provides several ideas to help students to avoid 'mismanaging' complexity. In particular, she argues that pupils should be helped:
>
> - to behave as writers, using all aspects of the process (composing, drafting, proof reading, etc.);
> - to build confidence by providing for the supportive and sympathetic contexts for writing;
> - to develop a knowledge of key grammatical concepts, e.g. subject, verb, object, indirect object and modifier, etc.
>
> Shaughnessy stresses that such knowledge is almost indispensable if teachers intend to talk to their students about their sentences. (Beard 2001)

Shaughnessy was involved with other researchers in exploring ways in which pupils could be made more aware of the possible structurings of text, without too much old-fashioned, specific teaching of grammar. From her findings she recommends especially activities that involve the following transformations, exercises which she believes may offer the closest thing to 'piano finger' activities for the inexperienced writer:

- changing simple sentences to complex sentences
- changing complex sentences to simple sentences
- changing simple sentences to compound sentences
- changing independent clauses to dependent clauses
- changing dependent clauses to independent clauses. (*ibid.*)

Lessons to be learned from the Technical Accuracy Project

In the Technical Accuracy Project, commissioned by the QCA in the late 1990s, Debra Myhill, Course Leader for Secondary English/Drama PGCE at Exeter University, had the opportunity to consider the detailed characteristics of A grade, C grade and F grade texts in GCSE English. This information was made available to teachers in *Improving Writing at Key Stages 3 and 4* (QCA 1999b) and is further explored in Myhill's very helpful book *Better Writers* (2001a).

The findings from the project cover a number of categories, but I shall confine my interest to clause structure, word classes and punctuation.

Clause structure

A grade candidates usually demonstrate:

- variety in sentences: simple and multiple;
- sentences expanded by the use of adverbials/non-finite clauses;
- considerably more subordination than coordination (the ability to link ideas by integrating clauses in complex sentences, rather than the excessive use of 'and' and 'then', etc.);
- effective use of subordination and coordination;
- varied subordinating/coordinating conjunctions.

Word classes

A grade candidates usually demonstrate:

- greater use of abstract nouns;
- greater lexical density (fewer words with purely syntactic or grammatical function such as auxiliary verbs, articles, prepositions, conjunctions; greater use of words that carry meaning such as nouns, adjectives, adverbs, main verbs);
- reduced number of finite verbs;
- greater use of adverbs of place.

Punctuation

A grade writers usually:

- are more accurate;
- include a variety of devices;
- use commas parenthetically;
- employ the omissive apostrophe correctly.

On the other hand, weaker writers have less knowledge of these characteristics, lack confidence in applying them in their own work, and have few mechanisms for self-improvement without the support of teachers pointing them to such aspects of remediation. For pupils of all abilities, these findings enable a linguistic focus to be applied to their work, and teachers should choose the most appropriate and necessary examples for their pupils to practise to improve the accuracy and interest of their work.

Each of these characteristics needs to be brought to the attention of pupils, so that they can work on increasing their own understanding of what they might do to improve their work. I have selected two features – 'stronger writers employ a greater number of abstract nouns, and fewer finite verbs' – for closer exploration.

Understanding and more confident use of abstract nouns

'*The calm of the landscape was captured in its silence and stillness. The blanket of heat causing inertia and tiredness.*' This example gives a strong impressionistic picture of place not always as powerfully replicated through the repeated use of adjectives which are often the alternative style chosen by less confident writers; for example: '*The landscape was calm, silent and still. Nothing moved and everything was still.*'

Pupils need to consider the relative value of abstract nouns in particular circumstances, such as their different uses and effects in fiction and non-fiction. The discussion of important ideas, for example, demands an understanding of the use of abstract nouns such as 'justice', 'democracy' and, more recently relevant, 'citizenship'. Having control of such words allows pupils to stand aside for a moment and reflect more broadly on concepts and broad ideas rather than rushing onwards. In some subjects of the school curriculum (e.g. history, geography, mathematics and science), the skill of *nominalisation* (making a noun or noun phrase from a word of another word class, such as a verb or an adjective) is a vital way of acquiring knowledge in these subjects. Thus, 'multiplication and subtraction' are essential requirements of mathematical knowledge; the 'Restoration' is the name of a period of English history, giving rise to conjecture about just what was 'restored'; 'erosion' is a central idea in physical geography, whilst 'carbonisation' matters a great deal to chemists (more astute pupils will notice the 'tion' at the ends of a number of these words, and already be pursuing related trains of thought). Encouraging and modelling their more frequent use in writing could be a possible way of improving the range of some writers' work, and an aid to developing their thinking through writing. George Keith often represents the most positive reasons for grammar study through the statement: 'Grammar is joined up thinking!' No other instance of grammar knowledge illustrates this saying more effectively than this example.

Encouraging pupils to reduce the use of finite verbs

Less fluent writers have a tendency to pile events on top of each other in an unstoppable, breathless way in their work. All teachers have encountered pupils who rush forward in a headlong manner, losing sight of any consideration of the characters involved or the purposes of their work. When uncertain of how to proceed in any task, these writers regularly choose the recount genre, which – at its most fundamental level – allows them to add these 'layers' of events without regard for the 'filling'; for example:

> We *went* down to the shops **and** *saw* our mates what *shall* we *do* billy *asked*. we *walked* to the hole by the railway. I *wanted* to go home no *come* with us said Billy, **and** he *went* in The others *climbed* in **and** they *went* down the bank, They *lifted* a big bit of wood on to the line. the train *was coming*.

This is writing at a fast pace, but with no real regard for the reader. The author offers no opinion, no descriptive detail. Without adjectives, the only real assistance offered about place or setting is through adverbial phrases of place: 'to the shops', 'by the railway', 'down the bank' and 'on to the line'. A disproportionate number of pronouns are employed and we do not gain a sense of any sort of recognisable person taking part. Writers who use this characteristic style need to be shown how they can ask questions of it for themselves, and how they can move through stages leading to improvement. They will need to know terms such as 'finite verb', 'coordinated clauses' and 'subordinated clauses' if they are to address the problems connected with those ideas.

Using picture books as models for writing

There is much to be learned from the uncomplicated writing of picture books, often believed to be more suitable for younger pupils, but actually written for any discriminating audience. (Surely any well-written text can be enjoyed by any audience; readers do not depend on the size of the printed text, or whether it is accompanied by pictures.)

> There are now sufficient good picture books on the market for teachers to provide eleven year olds as well as four year olds with very rich reading experiences. Although the text of these books is simple, the meaning behind them is not, and the older the child the greater their insight will be into the meaning. (Baddeley and Eddershaw 1994)

A further advantage of picture books in aiding pupils to focus on linguistic structure is that they are usually much shorter, and transmit their meanings more quickly and economically. Pupils of all abilities can be involved in quite sophisticated language-based study, as the example of Anthony Browne's *Voices in the Park* illustrated in the Introduction.

Pat Hutchins' famous book *Rosie's Walk* is a good text to begin picture book study. Pupils can be challenged to explain the structure of the text, and to use that knowledge as a writing 'frame' for a similar text of their own. The whole of Hutchins' original printed text is as follows:

> Rosie the hen went for a walk   across the yard
> around the pond
> over the haystack
> past the mill
> through the fence
> under the beehives
> and got back in time for dinner.
> (Hutchins 1968)

The pictures accompanying the written text add considerable meaning that would not be possible to convey in words. Pupils will recognise quite quickly, with a little probing, that the whole text is a single, compound sentence, the first half of which is extended by repetitive use of prepositional/adverbial phrases. Pupils will be able to suggest alternative versions of their own, for example:

> Last night I travelled home from school through the estate, across the main road, under the viaduct, behind the allotments and arrived home in time for *Neighbours*.

Not the most impressive prose, but more colourful and detailed than some pupils could construct on their own. (The separate phrases would also make pupils pay attention to the manner in which they should be separated, and suggest the use of commas in this context.)

Close consideration of a beautifully presented story, *Tortuga* by Paul Geraghty, offers a 'model' of another helpful linguistic device. The story begins with a lot of exciting action affecting the tortoise at its centre:

> Dark clouds blotted out the sun and the sky began to rumble. Tortuga took one look, then tucked into her shell. A big storm was coming. The wind whipped up the waves and bent the trees. Branches flew in the howling gale and soon whole trunks were ripped from the ground. (Geraghty 2000)

The opening sentences employ the most common sentence structure, SVO/A, where the elements making up the storm (the subjects of the sentences – 'dark clouds', 'the sky', 'a big storm', 'the wind', 'branches' and 'whole trunks') are cited, then immediately seen in action (the verbs – 'blotted', 'whipped', 'flew' and 'were ripped'). But on the next page of the story the mood of the narrative changes and the world becomes calmer. The sentence structure also changes at this point to mirror the new situation:

> When light returned, she found herself floating in the ocean. Heavy with eggs and aching with hunger, she drifted for days with nothing but waves and sky as far as the eye could see.

At this point, sentences no longer begin with the subject, but with adverbial phrases. It is as if the central character, the tortoise, is cushioned by these introductory phrases. Asking pupils to seek out other uses of the structuring of sentences, and to explain why they think they have been composed in that manner, could be a valuable way of ensuring that writers recognise the intrinsic relationship between structure and meaning. As Debra Myhill reminds us:

> many of the sentence level linguistic features had an effect upon the whole text. This underlines that it is difficult to separate mechanistically the 'surface features' of writing from the content, as is often the case. The way a text is written is intrinsically related to how successfully it communicates – what is written is affected by how it is written. (Myhill 2001a)

Many English departments have a module in their Key Stage 3 schemes of work that encourages their pupils to write a book for children in KS1.

Very often a class will be taken to an infant school to meet the prospective readers of these texts. What the adolescent authors sometimes learn is that books for young children will not be received favourably if the readers feel patronised by language that is too simple and undemanding. Good, focused linguistic study of popular young children's books will soon convince KS 3 pupils that such books are often very carefully constructed using a number of sophisticated devices.

Creating and using 'narrative writing frames'

In Chapter 3 there was a reference to how knowledge of the characteristics of different genres can assist pupils in writing more purposeful and effective prose. Much of the genre knowledge promoted by the primary Literacy Strategy is concerned with non-fiction texts. A training folder, *Literacy Across the Curriculum* (DfEE 2001e), published to support the implementation of Literacy Across the Curriculum in secondary schools as part of the Key Stage 3 Strategy, contains a valuable 17-page section illustrating the grammatical features of non-fiction texts necessary for pupils to employ in different subjects of the secondary curriculum. There is virtually nothing of the same scale to enable teachers to support pupils in attempting to compose narrative texts.

One way of addressing this omission would be for English departments (which, after all, give more attention to narrative writing than do most other subject departments) to establish their own 'narrative writing frames'. Pupils would need to be familiar with a collection of passages from, for instance, a range of action adventure or suspense texts. Careful reading of these passages would be likely to reveal that *action adventure* texts regularly comprise the following features:

- a crush of verbs
- generous use of adverbial and adjectival phrases
- variable sentence/paragraph length – occasionally very short for closely focused effect
- frequent commas
- unfinished sentences – ellipsis
- frequent exclamations
- breathless, hurried dialogue
- inner turmoil, possibly expressed through monologue
- impressionistic senses of events and setting, rather than clear pictures
- a rush of images.

Similarly, samples of *suspense writing* are likely to display a larger proportion of the following aspects:

- short, punchy sentences
- one word used as a 'sentence'
- adverbs often the first word of a sentence
- sentence structuring changed (e.g. 'Before. . .', 'To their surprise. . .', 'At that moment. . .', etc.
- facts are hidden from the reader in less specific vocabulary – 'it', 'something', 'the thing'
- reactions of characters often denoted through their actions, not description (verbs, not adjectives)
- the writer might ask questions
- use of linguistic effects – personification/metaphor/simile – to create pictures and effects.

If pupils have actually created these sorts of 'frames' for themselves, with suitable and helpful teacher guidance and support, they will feel much more in tune with the features they have discovered. They could then be asked to write a few sentences, or even a few paragraphs, of the relevant type of narrative, including specifically a number of these characteristics – and be expected to explain what the addition of such a feature has contributed to the overall meaning of the passage.

The examples illustrated above are not offered as the only possibilities of such types of text; English departments are challenged to come up with better, more detailed lists of their own. There are only two sorts of narrative genre explored in this example; departments could also consider and construct suitable 'frames' for such areas as: horror; science fiction; romance; comedy; historical narrative; fantasy; fable or legend – or any others in which the English team might be interested. Depending on the ability of the pupils, teachers will be able to make differentiated demands on the number of criteria to be included in examples of each type, and also the quality of those examples. Such an approach, however, does allow teachers to be specific in the requirements they make about writing tasks, which can be more helpful for less confident writers, and link the assessment closely to the task.

Playing with genre

Having enabled pupils to pay closer attention to the language of different sorts of texts, it is only a short step to encouraging pupils into 'games and exercises' using different genres to consolidate their new knowledge. This sort of exercise may be conducted initially with non-fiction texts if pupils are less sure of what to do, but can be equally valuable when applied to narrative genres.

One of the easier non-fiction texts to teach is the instructional or procedural text. These are usually very straightforward. As explained in Chapter 3 they 'front' *verbs* in a pronounced way, because they are concerned essentially with bringing about a result of some focused activity. Pupils can be supported in seeing how frequently verbs are at work, and the relationship of collections of verbs associated with similar activities. Thus a recipe book might instruct prospective chefs to 'rub', 'mix', 'sieve', 'cut', 'peel', 'pour', 'knead', 'roll', 'decorate', etc., while a book instructing the budding artist how to paint will use words such as 'look', 'sketch', 'draw', 'shade', 'mix', 'spread', 'darken', 'outline', etc. Verbs typical of a mechanical repair manual might be 'locate', 'press', 'turn', 'release', 'wipe', 'screw', 'adjust', 'test', 'select', etc. Teachers could set up short writing tasks on different sorts of instructional contexts, challenging their pupils to locate and identify the verbs characteristic of those activities.

Having gained a secure knowledge of which linguistic features might appear most often in one sort of text type, pupils could be shown how to move from one text type to another:

- An explanation of how digestion works might be transformed into an instruction to the food passing through the body to undergo certain processes in the gut.
- A piece of non-chronological writing about the natural habitats of particular mammals – the material of natural history books – could be changed into a persuasion text, making overblown claims for certain sorts of moss, or the obvious superior qualities of one sort of craggy rock over another.
- A recount of an event can be stripped down to its most fundamental details, then built up again into a number of alternative narratives possibly depicting fear, suggesting mystery or headily descriptive.

Contexts can be changed:

- The recounting of a chemistry experiment could be undertaken in completely the wrong style, with quite inappropriate and irrelevant detail (e.g. The tall, handsome teacher gently lifted a shining, freshly washed glass beaker, the light reflecting from it in a rainbow of colours, etc.).
- An emotional event written wholly as a set of biological phenomena.
- A formal argument written in colloquial terms.

In all these instances, pupils would have to pay close attention to the grammatical effects they are subverting and playing with. The *Guardian* has a regular feature in its Saturday 'Editor' section where a recently published novel is summarised and reviewed in the style of the original. This sort of exercise is an excellent way of modelling for pupils ways of noticing the chief and prevailing features of language.

Fiction texts can be changed for the same grammar learning ends:

- A nursery rhyme could be made into a short story.
- A fairy story could be turned into a newspaper article.
- A love story could be changed into a crime situation; an action narrative transformed into a reflective piece; a passage of prose – without dialogue – rewritten as a set of play directions or a cinema/television screenplay.
- Formal biblical passages could be rewritten for young readers.
- A passage from Shakespeare could be updated in the style of characters from different modes of modern life.

The example of writing given in Box 6.1 was produced by a very able girl who was bored with producing straightforward narrative fiction. She was challenged to write a continuous narrative that passed through a number of genres, some offering specific difficulties. The result demonstrated not only a real assurance with narrative style, but also a close acquaintance with different genres and forms of text.

Exploring the use of adjectives in different settings

Pupils can benefit from realising that words work differently in different text-type contexts. A good example of work that teachers can promote to make this understanding clearer could be undertaken with *adjectives*.

- In **persuasive** texts there is usually a piling up of adjectives;
  e.g. A *mouthwatering* feast of *fine Scottish* cuisine, prepared by *award winning* chefs – that's the experience awaiting you from—. The *freshest* of Scottish produce – all *additive-free* – is transformed into *delicious* meals, carefully prepared and made to order for you by our *expert Gourmet* chefs. Chilled immediately and packed for delivery, your order is despatched overnight to arrive at your door in *perfect* condition the very *next* day.
  There are 12 adjectives in this piece which is 69 words long – between one-fifth and one-sixth of the whole passage.

Box 6.1 Example of writing

The Reivers

Diary of Petra Carrson
14th March 1595

Rumour has it that the Reivers are coming soon! I go all shivery as I write the words. A neighbouring farmer galloped over to tell us this morning. When Mother heard, she covered her face with her hands and ran from the table, crying. I started to shake and Papa held me on his lap like he did when I was little. When I had eventually calmed down, he told me to fetch some milk from the dairy. I did but when I was walking back, I heard a distressed servant shouting 'They'll be here tomorra neet!' and gasps from the listeners. As I heard this my knees collapsed beneath me, I heard the thud as my head hit the floor and everything went black.

A school history book

During the years 1500 to 1650, terrible robbing gangs roamed the border country between England and Scotland. They were called Reivers. They attacked or reived houses and stole food, clothes and animals. Several stories exist today about their frightening activities. One well-known raid was when the Carrson house was attacked. The Reivers set the Carrson house on fire and stole everything of value. Then, when the grandfather Armstrong attempted to stop them, he was shot. The rest of the family then escaped to Tullie House in Carlisle where they lived for six months, before moving to and settling in Manchester. A museum can be found in Carlisle today in Mr James Tullie's name. If you are ever in the area, you may want to discover more about these events.

Tullie House
Carlisle
Cumberland

31st March 1595

My dearest Margaret,

I write to you in deepest sorrow. As you will gather from the address, we are lodging at Tullie House, the reason being that not long ago the Reivers (I shudder to write this) destroyed our house by fire. Before they came (we heard news of their coming) we managed to pack a few necessities and flee.

But then the Reivers arrived! They sang a victory song and set our great house and the surrounding buildings alight with blazing torches. We were terrified and paralysed by their power.

Poor Papa. He was killed in the most cowardly way, when he staggered out of the burning house. He threatened the Reivers with swords, but they shot him with muskets. I sobbed and shrieked over Papa and covered myself with his blood when I sat him up and hugged him. I placed his granddaughter, Clara, in his arms and shouted curses at the Reivers. Then I escaped into the night with Peter and the children.

Box 6.1 continued

The rest of us struggled on, through bad weather, especially very fierce storms. The children were constantly frightened and Clara contracted fever, poor thing. She nearly died of choking, as we cowered in a hedge. After two weeks of struggle, we had entered the town of Carlisle and were taken in by an old friend, a kind man by name of Mr James Tullie. We are now living in his happy home. It is our intention to escape the border area.

Yours dearly,
Anne

The Daily Border

Carrson Home Destroyed in Raid

Late on the night of 13th March, the Carrson house was attacked by Reivers. Apparently, according to the mother, Mrs Anne Carrson, they approached on horseback at the dead of night.

The grandfather, Osbert Armstrong, was shot dead when trying to halt the evil deeds of the attacking Reivers. The Reivers stole horses, cattle, food, money and jewellery. They burnt the house to the ground and then left at approximately two o'clock.

The rest of the family are currently lodged at Mr James Tullie's house in Carlisle, to which they escaped on that fateful night. No-one else was hurt, but Anne Carson's two year old daughter, Clara, has a severe fever. The whole family are suffering from severe shock.

The Carrson and Armstrong families are respected ones in this area, especially Osbert Armstrong who lived in his house for eighty four years. The family was joined to the Carrsons when Peter Carrson married Anne Armstrong, as reported in this journal 14 years ago. The house was an extensive one, richly appointed, with many servants, but it has suffered cruelly from the fire deliberately caused by the murderous intruders. Sadly, it now stands ruined and derelict. Since the disaster the family have been trying to plan settling down to normal family life in another part of England.

Diary of Petra Carrson
10th October 1595

I am writing this diary entry in the nursery that I share with Clara in our new home in Manchester. On 21st September, we left Tullie House and started our journey to the new house that Papa has bought. Glory be! Tonight I can go to bed and feel secure in the knowledge that I can sleep until the morning sun shines on my face. Today I went to fetch milk. I spent the whole journey enjoying the safety of the town. Tomorrow I shall get out of bed and rush outside and greet the morning and my new life that awaits me.

or:

This *classy*, *versatile* notebook makes working on the move a pleasure – combining *effortless* power and *DRR* memory. Plus *Microsoft*® Windows® XP₁₀ to ensure that you have everything you need for *true* mobility at *low* cost.

- In fairy stories the adjectives are performing important 'framing' functions and are usually very simple and uncomplicated, because their task is to make an effect on young readers; e.g.
  the *wicked* stepmother, the *good* fairy, the *poor* miller, the *handsome* prince, the *ugly* sister, the *brave* hero and the *cruel* giant.
- Adjectives in recipes matter a great deal, and have to convey an accuracy vital to the successful outcome of the cooking; e.g.
  whip until *fluffy*, cook until *brown*, add *one* fluid ounce, pour into a *flat* dish.

Some pupils believe that their work will be improved by adding indiscriminate numbers of adjectives. It is not unusual, in writing exercises taking place in primary classrooms, to hear teachers urging their pupils to 'make sure there are plenty of adjectives, to make it more interesting for your readers'. In fact, careful employment of appropriate adjectives is a far more controlled manner of writing. Debra Myhill, from her research into pupils' writing, informs us that weaker writers often neglect adjectives, middle-range writers rely too heavily on them, and the best writers move beyond them!

Using and practising a range of connectives

All young people use connectives quite naturally in their work without giving them a second thought. Knowing that they are using connectives for particular sorts of 'joined-up thinking' could be yet another way whereby pupils take more control of their written work.

Teachers and pupils may not always be familiar with the notion of 'connectives' (although pupils who have enjoyed careful and supportive teaching in their primary Literacy Hours should be more knowledgeable about their functions). Teachers who are not so aware of the changes in modern grammar will undoubtedly know what conjunctions are, but not necessarily 'connectives'. If readers refer to the 'map of grammar' (see Figure 4.1) they will recall the two parts of grammar – the phrase generators and the clause generators. In between these two essential elements, on which base all ideas are constructed, are the 'fasteners' of language – the connectors. These apparently unimportant ingredients of language actually have the power to signal all sorts of degrees of meaning, requiring pupils to give them concentrated attention. They should never, however (that is a connective in action!), be studied in a dry, decontextualised manner (any more than all the other recommended grammar work in this book). Nevertheless (another one!), classrooms can offer more support by being used to display lists of connectives, and teachers should remind pupils to include them appropriately to add an extra dimension to their work. A number of connectives, appropriate for particular contexts, are given in Table 6.1, and these could be displayed to support pupils' writing. Teachers could suggest that pupils incorporate lesser known examples in their writing, pointing out how effective they can be in the construction of certain types of discourse not possible without this extent of vocabulary.

Connectives may be words or phrases. They are probably learned most easily when explored by pupils in different text types, where they may be seen to be performing different functions.

In *recount texts*, for example, the connectives are significant for the manner in which they move the piece on, giving a chronological sequence to the events:

Last week our class went on a journey to Woburn Abbey. The coach took an hour to reach the Abbey, and when we arrived, we had lunch. *After that*, we went to the main house to be shown around. *Later*, the guide showed us the secret passage at the back of the house. *At four o' clock*, we had tea, *and then* we went back to the buses.

These simple devices help to relate what went on during the trip.

In *explanation texts* the connectives will be making relationships between the events in a causal manner, usually in sequence too:

The rocks which make up the ocean floor are all young – nowhere older than 200 million years. *This is because* new ocean plate is constantly being made by volcanic eruptions deep below the ocean waters. A long range of mountains snakes through the oceans, cut at its heart by a rift valley. The volcanoes in this rift valley erupt constantly producing new rock. *Under the huge pressure of the ocean water*, the lava erupts gently, like toothpaste squeezed from a tube, to form rounded shapes known as pillow lava. The new rock fills in the widening rift as the plates pull apart. *In this way* . . . (Van Rose 1992)

A few final writing challenges in which pupils can practise and improve their grammatical knowledge and control

Turning active prose into the passive voice
This speaks largely for itself. Pupils are encouraged to attempt passages of writing where they move from the familiar active voice to the more indirect

Table 6.1 Connectives – useful words and phrases

Addition	Sequence	Illustration	Cause and effect	Persuasion	Contrast and balance	Comparison	Opinion and interpretation
and also further (more) in addition too again the following and then what is more moreover as well as as a corollary to complement	initially first(ly) then so far after(wards) at last (lastly) finally once secondly (etc.) next subsequently meanwhile at length in the end eventually succeeding following since prior to previously later to begin with	for example for instance such as as as revealed by thus to show that to take the case of to elucidate that is to say in other words a case in point an instance	consequently thus so hence as a result because/as therefore accordingly since/until whenever as long as effectively of course depending upon necessarily eventually inevitably it may happen that in the course of things	of course naturally obviously clearly evidently surely certainly decidedly indeed virtually no wonder strangely enough oddly enough luckily (un)fortunately admittedly undoubtedly	but however nevertheless alternatively to turn to yet despite this on the contrary as for the opposite still instead on the other hand (on the one hand) whereas otherwise although apart from equally to balance this compensating for this all the same for all that albeit/though taking one thing with another it is doubtful confuting this/disputing this	equally similarly compared with (in comparison) comparatively an equivalent in the same way likewise as with to balance (this) in juxtaposition by way of contrast in contrast	it would seem one might consider/ suggest/ propose/ deduce/infer imagine/ conclude presumably in the view of on the strength of to the best of one's belief theoretically literally obviously possibly maybe contrary to improbably incredibly

Summary (Addition)
in brief
in short
on the whole
throughout
in all
overall
to sum up
in summary
to recapitulate
in a nutshell
in conclusion

Emphasis (Illustration)
above all
in particular
notably
specifically
especially
significantly
more importantly
indeed
explicitly
in fact

Conclusion (Persuasion)
to conclude
in conclusion
after all
finally
when all is said and done
in the end
ultimately

Restriction (Comparison)
only if
unless
except (for)
save (for)

passive voice. Perhaps they might attempt a diary entry in the active voice; then one in the passive form.

- *Active*: I spent the day playing computer games with my friend. We played a really wicked game most of the morning. I had my dinner there, and watched telly when I got home.
- *Passive*: It was decided that I had to stay in all day. Rain was pouring down the whole time. The weather made me really fed up. It will be worse tomorrow.

Turning a piece of conversational writing into a formal passage

Pupils should be asked to construct a piece of dialogue, or even an extended monologue. They do not need to go to the extent of setting it out in the form of a play script, but they should try to capture the sense of hesitation and repetition characteristic of speech. The same discourse should then be written in formal prose in an attempt to capture the 'flavour' of the original, but dealt with in standard English.

Working on from grammatically recognisable fragments

Offer pupils snatches of well-known text, and ask them to construct at least an extract of a whole piece containing that fragment:

- . . . horrified to discover. . .
- . . . a gripping human drama. . .
- . . . is an unparalleled. . .
- . . . In a far off kingdom. . .
- . . . when the mixture was poured into. . .
- . . . this is the last time. . .
- . . . The star later commented. . .

Writing familiar sorts of texts in unfamiliar situations

Pupils can be encouraged to write in ways that are commonplace in the world, but that deal with unusual contents:

- they might be encouraged to 'sell' their brothers and sisters in the style of a house agent's flyer;
- they might be encouraged to write about a sandwich lunch as if it is a gourmet meal;
- they might describe a member of staff as if writing about a film star in a teenage girls' magazine;
- they might describe the view from their bedroom window as if it has appeared in a travel brochure;

- they might describe a journey on the school bus as if it is a review in a motoring magazine.

Considering how the opening of a text determines the eventual direction it will take – and thinking of alternatives

This idea is 'borrowed' from an article in *The Secondary English Magazine* by Nicholas McGuinn, which in turn is based on an exercise in George Keith and John Shuttleworth's book *Living Language* (1997).

Pupils are encouraged to pay considerable attention to the openings of sentences because, as Keith and Shuttleworth (1997) argue:

> These words have considerable structural significance since they will determine to a large extent the overall shape of a sentence.

McGuinn develops this idea in relation to professionally produced persuasive texts, which he claims:

> use a subtle range of rhetorical strategies to achieve the desired effect. They cajole, flatter, frighten, wheedle, joke, look for sympathy, exaggerate – and so on. Above all – and this is the crucial point – they disguise themselves as something else.

So, to help pupils recognise the potential of sentences and the ways they can proceed, he takes the beginning of a persuasive text:

The Po valley

The first stage of the exercise is to invite students to speculate about the kind of text this might be. There are positive opportunities here for productive word level work: what clues, we might ask, do the use of the determiner and the capital letter provide? Moving outwards to consider issues of intertextuality, we can think about the implications of the geographical reference: what images, associations does it evoke?

The next stage is to explore the concept of the 'grammatical flight path' by trying to write an ending to the sentence. Here are some possible responses:

The Po valley lies in the north of Italy.
The Po valley, nestling in the foothills of the mighty Alps, must surely rank as one of Italy's most famous and attractive tourist destinations.
The Po valley! So that's what Edgar had meant when, with his dying breath, he held her close and whispered: 'Italy!'

The pupils are then asked to look at the original text, which actually begins: '*The Po valley became*...', thereby invalidating any of the options attempted above! Rather than a geographically based text, the writer is now moving into a historical context. So how might the sentence develop if the opening phrase is followed by 'is' or 'could' or 'might' or 'will' – or other alternatives?

Such exercises, which are probably more suitable for able writers, focus a strong intensity on thinking about how sentences can possibly take shape, and the constraints that certain choices, at particular points, can bring.

Conclusion

I have offered a tiny fraction of possible ways to engage young writers in exploring and demonstrating their huge potential for language knowledge in writing tasks. Teachers should continue to be urged to use their considerable creative talents so often evident in good English classrooms, illustrated here in typical enthusiastic style by Geoff Barton in the *TES*, to bring about exciting and progressive writing development:

Start with something active – a question, puzzle, activity, mystery text. Best of all use a question to kick-start the exploration:

- How do writers build suspense?
- How do writers tell stories from different points of view?
- How do advertisers of products that are really tacky persuade us that we cannot live without them?

Next look at a sample text. The best texts are short and pithy: a snippet from a brochure or leaflet, a cutting from the *Daily Mail* editorial, the instructions on how to programme your video. Arid analysis will not work. Students have to explore the text actively. So write it for a different audience – someone who has owned a video previously, or for someone who is not even sure how to open the box. Make it more personal. Make it more impersonal. Make it chatty. Set the instructions out in a continuous prose paragraph. Change them to bullet points. Add more description. Cut all the description. Make the verbs more active. Tell the whole thing using diagrams and labels. (Barton 2001)

English departments should seek to discover something of the same excitement and pleasure in engaging their pupils in grammar-based/ linguistically focused work as is illustrated in this sort of attitude.

Postscript

The following texts contain much more detailed knowledge than this book could hope to cover about specific aspects of grammar helpful to any secondary teacher. Most also contain full glossaries of grammatical and linguistic terminology.

George Keith, *Learning about Language (Teacher's Resource)*. Hodder and Stoughton (2001).
Beverley Derewianka, *A Grammar Companion for Primary Teachers*. PETA, W. Australia (1998). Don't be put off by the title of this book; it is not easy to obtain, but PETA has a website: **www.edu.au**.
John Collerson, *English Grammar – A Functional Approach*. PETA (1994).
David Crystal, *Language A to Z – 1 & 2*. Longman (1991).
Geoff Barton, *Grammar in Context*. Oxford University Press (1999).
David Crystal, *The Cambridge Encyclopaedia of Language*. Cambridge University Press (1988).

If you can still obtain or borrow a LINC folder, there is still much valuable material to be found in it.
For really technical explanations of language, I have found Howard Jackson's *Grammar and Meaning* (Longman 1990) extremely useful.

Bibliography

References

Allen, N. (2002) 'Too much, too young? An analysis of the key stage 3 National Literacy Strategy in practice', *English in Education*, **36**(1), 5–15.

Bain, R., Fitzgerald, B. and Taylor, M. (eds) (1992) *Looking into Language.* London: Hodder & Stoughton.

Barton, G. (1998) 'Grammar without shame', *The Use of English*, **42**(2), 107–18.

Barton, G. (2001) 'Unexpected genres', *TES Curriculum Special*, 9 February.

Beard, R. (2000) *Developing Writing.* London: Hodder & Stoughton.

Beard, R. (2001) *The Effective Teaching of Writing.* 'NFER topic' series. Slough: NFER.

Black, P. and Wiliam, D. (1998) *Inside the Black Box.* London: Kings College.

Bleiman, B. (1999) 'Integrating language and literature at A level', *The English & Media Magazine*, **40**, 19–22.

Bridley, S. (ed.) (1994) *Teaching English.* London: Routledge.

Bullock, A. (1974) *A Language for Life.* London: HMSO.

Burgess, T. (2002) 'Writing, English teachers and the new professionalism', in Ellis, V. (ed.) *'When the Hurly Burly's Done': What's Worth Fighting for in English Education?* Sheffield: NATE.

Carter, R. (ed.) (1990) *Knowledge about Language and the Curriculum: The LINC Reader.* London: Hodder & Stoughton.

Clarke, S. (2001) *Unlocking Formative Assessment.* London: Hodder & Stoughton.

Collerson, J. (1994) *English Grammar: A Functional Approach.* NSW, Australia: PETA.

Collerson, J. (1997) *Grammar in Teaching.* NSW, Australia: PETA.

Cox, B. (1991) *Cox on Cox: An English Curriculum for the 1990s.* London: Hodder & Stoughton.

Cox, B. (1994) 'The right is wrong on English teaching', *The Times*, 22 June.

Crystal, D. (1987) *The Cambridge Encyclopaedia of Language.* Cambridge: Cambridge University Press.

D'Arcy, P. (n.d.) *Two Contrasting Paradigms for the Teaching and the Assessment of Writing.* Sheffield: NATE/NAAE/NAPE.

D'Arcy, P. (2001) 'A comparison between two kinds of response, interpretive and skill-based, to a Year 6 story "Three Wishes"', *English in Education*, **36**(2), 40–9.

Davies, C. (2000) '"Correct" or "appropriate"?', in Davison, J. and Moss, J. (eds) *Issues in English Teaching*. London: Routledge.

Dean, G. (2000) *Teaching Reading in Secondary Schools*. London: David Fulton.

Dean, G. (2002) *Teaching English in the Key Stage 3 Literacy Strategy*. London: David Fulton.

Derewianka, B. (1990) *Exploring How Texts Work*. NSW, Australia: PETA.

Derewianka, B. (1998) *A Grammar Companion for Primary Teachers*. NSW, Australia: PETA.

DES (1984) *English from 5 to 16 – Curriculum Matters 1*. London: HMSO.

DES (1986) *English from 5 to 16 – The Response to Curriculum Matters 1*. London: HMSO.

DfEE (1998) *The National Literacy Strategy Module 2 – Word Level Work. Teacher's notes Unit 1: Introduction*. London: DfEE.

DES (1988) *Report of the Committee of Inquiry into the Teaching of English Language*. London: HMSO.

DfEE/SEU (2001a) *Key Stage 3 National Strategy – Framework for Teaching English: Years 7, 8 & 9*. London: DfEE.

DfEE/SEU (2001b) *Year 7 Sentence Level Bank*. London: DfEE.

DfEE/SEU (2001c) *English Department Training 2001*. London: DfEE.

DfEE/SEU (2001d) *Year 7 Spelling Bank*. London: DfEE.

DfEE/SEU (2001e) *Literacy Across the Curriculum*. London: DfEE.

DfEE (1998) The National Literacy Strategy Module 2 – Word Level Work. Teacher's notes Unit 1: Introduction. London: DfEE.

Ellis, V. (ed.) (2002) *'When the Hurly Burly's Done': What's Worth Fighting for in English Education?* Sheffield: NATE.

Frater, G. (2000) *Securing Boys' Literacy*. London: Basic Skills Agency.

Hall, C. and Coles, M. (1999) *Children's Reading Choices*. London: Routledge.

Halliday, M. (1978) *Language as Social Semiotic*. London: Arnold.

Harrison, C. (2002) *Key Stage 3 English – Roots and Research*. London: DfES.

Hillocks, G. (1986) *Research on Written Composition*. Urbana, IL: National Conference on Research English/ERIC Clearinghouse on Reading and Communication Skills.

Hillocks, G. (1995) *Teaching Writing as Reflective Practice*. New York: Teachers College Press.

Hilton, M. (2001) 'Writing process and progress', *English in Education*, **35**, 4–11.

Keith, G. (1997) 'Teach yourself English grammar', *The English & Media Magazine*, **36**, 8–12.

Keith, G. (1999) 'Noticing grammar', in *Not Whether But How* London: QCA.

Keith, G. (2001) *Learning about Language – Teacher's Resource*. London: Hodder & Stoughton.

Keith, G. and Shuttleworth, J. (1997) *Living Language: Exploring Advanced Level English*. London: Hodder & Stoughton.

Kress, G. (1989) 'Texture and meaning', in Andrews, R. (ed.) *Narrative and Argument*. Milton Keynes: Open University Press.

Kress, G. (1995) *Writing the Future*. Sheffield: NATE.

LINC (1992) *Language in the National Curriculum – Materials for Professional Development*. Nottingham: University of Nottingham.

Littlefair, A. (1991) *Reading All Types of Writing*. Buckingham: Open University Press.

Lodge, J. and Evans, P. (1995) 'How do we teach grammar?', in Protherough, R. and King, P. (eds) *The Challenge of English in the National Curriculum*. London: Routledge.

MacDonald, I. (2000) 'Time to go our separate ways', *TES*, 6 October.

McGuinn, N. (2002) 'Teaching the techniques of persuasion', *The Secondary English Magazine*, **5**(5), 29–32.

Marenbon, J. (1987) *English Our English*. London: Centre for Policy Studies.

Marshall, R. (2002) 'Editorial: Revolting literacy', *English in Education*, **36**(2), 1–6.

Martin, J. (1989) *Factual Writing: Exploring and Challenging Social Reality* (2nd edn). Oxford: Oxford University Press.

Mittins, B. (1988) *English: Not the Naming of Parts*. Sheffield: NATE.

Myhill, D. (2001a) *Better Writers*. Westley, Suffolk: Courseware Publications.

Myhill, D. (2001b) 'Writing: crafting and creating', *English in Education*, **35**(3), 13–20.

NCC (1992) *National Curriculum English: The Case for Revising the Order*. York: NCC.

Peim, N. (2000) 'The cultural politics of English teaching', in Davison, J. and Moss, J. (eds) *Issues in English Teaching*. London: Routledge.

Pope, R. (1998) *The English Studies Book*. London: Routledge.

Poulson, L. (1998) *The English Curriculum in Schools*. London: Cassell.

Pullman, P. (2002) *Perverse, All Monstrous, All Prodigious Things*. 'Perspectives on English Teaching' Series. Sheffield: NATE.

QCA (1997) *English Grammar, Spelling and Punctuation – Sample Test Materials*. London: QCA.

QCA (1998) *The Grammar Papers – Perspectives on the Teaching of Grammar in the National Curriculum*. London: QCA.

QCA (1999a) *Not Whether But How – Teaching Grammar in English at Key Stages 3 and 4*. London: QCA.

QCA (1999b) *Improving Writing at Key Stages 3 and 4*. London: QCA.

Quirk, R. *et al.* (1972) *A Grammar of Contemporary English*. London: Longman.

Richmond, J. (1992) 'Unstable materials', *The English & Media Magazine*, **26**, 13–18.

Rosen, M. (2002) 'Why grammar won't help – and what's really important about language and literature', in Taylor, P. (ed.) *Hard Times for English Teaching*. Leicester: SHA.

Saunders, M. (1976) *Developments in English Teaching*. London: Open Books.

Shaughnessy, M. (1977) *Errors and Expectations: A Guide for the Teacher of Basic Writing*. New York: Open University Press.

Watkins, G. (1973) 'Language teaching', in Hemington, R. *et al.* (eds) *The Teaching of English in Secondary Schools.* Cambridge: Cambridge University Press.

Wray, D. and Lewis, M. (1997) *Extending Literacy: Children Reading and Writing Non-fiction.* London: Routledge.

Textbooks, children's reading books and other references in the book

Almond, D. (1998) *Skellig.* London: Hodder Signature.

Baddeley, P. and Eddershaw, C. (1994) *Not so Simple Picture Books.* Stoke-on-Trent: Trentham Books.

Breslin, T. (2002) *Remembrance.* London: Doubleday.

Browne, A. (1977) *A Walk in the Park.* London: Picturemac, Macmillan.

Browne, A. (1998) *Voices in the Park.* London: Doubleday.

Clements, S., Dixon, J. and Stratta, L. (1963) *Reflections.* London: Oxford University Press.

Davies, S. (2001) *A–Z of Cult Films and Film-makers.* London: Batsford.

Dickinson, P. (1988) *Eva.* London: Corgi Freeway.

Doherty, B. (1991) *Dear Nobody.* London: Lions Tracks.

Geraghty, P. (2000) *Tortuga.* London: Red Fox.

Howarth, L. (1994) *Maphead.* London: Walker Books.

Howker, J. (1994) *Martin Farrell.* London: Red Fox.

Hutchins, P. (1968) *Rosie's Walk.* New York: Scholastic Press.

Mark, J. (2000) *heathrow nights.* London: Hodder Signature.

Newbery, L. (2001) *The Damage Done.* London: Scholastic Press.

O'Malley, R. and Thompson, D. (1955) *English One to Five.* London: Heinemann.

Pratchett, T. (1989) *Truckers.* London: Doubleday.

Pullman, P. (1996) *Clockwork.* London: Corgi Yearling.

Ridout, R. (1947) *English Today 2.* London: Ginn.

Rowe, A. and Emmens, P. (1963) *English Through Experience.* London: Blond Educational.

Sacher, L. (1998) *Holes.* London: Bloomsbury.

Smith, D. (2001) *Delia's How to Cook, Book Three.* London: BBC.

Snickert, L. (1999) *The Bad Beginning – Book the First.* New York: Harper Collins.

Swindells, R. (1993) *Stone Cold.* London: Puffin.

Van Rose, S. (1992) *Volcano.* London: Eyewitness Guides, Dorling Kindersley.

Wright, W. (1961) *A Basic Course in English.* Welwyn: Nisbet.

Zephaniah, B. (1999) *face.* London: Bloomsbury.

Magazine articles

Good Housekeeping (1998) 'Great summer escapes'. July.

Radio Times (2002) 14–20 September.

Index